STRATEGIC
Whitetail
HUNTING

TIM HOOEY

©2004 by Tim Hooey
Published by

krause publications
An imprint of F+W Publications, Inc.

**700 East State Street • Iola, WI 54990-0001
715-445-2214 • 888-457-2873
www.krause.com**

Our toll-free number to place an order or obtain
a free catalog is (800) 258-0929.

Library of Congress Catalog Number: 2004093882

ISBN: 0-87349-789-9

Designed by Paul Birling
Edited by Joel Marvin

Printed in United States

ABOUT THE AUTHOR

As host of the popular *North American Fish & Game* television program, Michigan's Tim Hooey has had the opportunity to hunt deer all over the United States and Canada. He has taken more than 150 whitetail bucks in his lifetime, using the techniques outlined in the following pages. An airline pilot by trade, Tim has recently signed on as Gander Mountain's newest pro-staff member. He lives in Michigan with his wife Joanne and children Rachel, Tara and Sean.

CONTENTS

DEDICATION

Strategic Whitetail Hunting could never have been written without the support and encouragement of my family. This book is dedicated to them. To my father, John Hooey, who helped me take my first steps as a hunter. To my mother, Barbara, who put up with a youngster who never made it to a family meal on time. To my wonderful spouse, Joanne, who becomes the ultimate hunting widow each season and whose devotion has helped my dreams become a reality. To my children, Rachel, Tara and Sean, whom I love more than deer hunting . . . and God only knows how much I love deer hunting. To each and every one, thank you.

Michigan's Tim Hooey has been hunting with a bow and a gun since he was 10 years old. His show North American Fish and Game *is nationally televised and his seminars have become extremely popular because they teach the confidence and fundamentals of hunting big, mature deer.*

FOREWORD

This is the golden age of hunting. The whitetail population in the U.S. has never been larger and with only a few exceptions, the deer herd has never been healthier.

I have had the great gift of hunting throughout North America for deer and bear, for pronghorns and sheep, and find that even for wonderful exotic game animals, the cost is bearable ... if I am okay with driving an older car and putting off the addition to the house. I do not mind.

So, what is holding you back?

My Michigan friend Tim Hooey is a terrific whitetail hunter. He is nuts about antlers and in his new book, *Strategic Whitetail Hunting,* he outlines a formula for hunting success that applies coast-to-coast. "Big whitetails live in your neighborhood," he says. "Stop killing little deer and commit yourself to taking only mature deer. Broaden your horizons. If you are passionate about big deer, you will put them on the table and on the wall." He is right.

Do not wait to get motivated, though. Do not wait until after the Super Bowl. Do not wait until the kids are off to college. This golden age will not last forever. The human population of North America is increasing rapidly and the cost of hunting creeps up every year. Most people are clueless about the food in their grocery store: "Who grows those cute cherry tomatoes and those tender little veal cutlets?"

Make up your mind to be a part of a wonderful tradition. Right now. Get off the sofa and make a commitment to yourself. Right now. You will never be sorry.

I will see you on the trail.

Bob Robb
Eagle River, Alaska
January 2004

INTRODUCTION

Believe that you can take big deer every year.

I hunted white-tailed deer when there were not many deer around. No, I did not score on a trophy rack every year when I started, but I always scored on a trophy, especially when I was bowhunting. Especially when I was a kid.

Trophy? Well, that's in the eyes of the beholder, isn't it?

Sure, I dreamed about deer with huge racks when I was a young-un growing up in New Jersey, but I did not see many. Relatively speaking, they were as rare then as they are now when the whitetail population in North America is two or three times as large as it was in the '60s.

Now we live in the 21st century and during the past four decades, I have hunted my butt off with a gun, a bow and blackpowder. If hunting with a spear were legal in most places, I would learn that, too. So, I've taken a lot of deer with a gun and bow. A few of them had big racks, but all of them were trophies. Really.

I have gotten older and the deer seem to have gotten smarter. Well, go figure. However, I have gotten smarter, too, at last!

It also seems that there are a lot more hunters searching for big deer today, and I don't mean deer with heavy bodies, like two-hundred-pounders. Heck. The way we hunters talk today, it occasionally sounds like deer don't need bodies at all. All that matters to some of our new breed of "trophy hunter" is that deer have horns. Big horns. Book horns.

So, when I travel to give a seminar or meet other hunters in the field while I'm filming a segment for *North American Fish & Game,* guys always get around to asking, "What do I have to do to take big bucks every year?"

Have you ever asked anyone that question … or even asked yourself? Are you too self-conscious? Hunting is kind of a macho thing after all, and if you haven't taken big racks consistently … well, what does THAT say about you? Have you ever seriously wondered why YOU don't take mature deer, a big buck or even a dominant doe, every year? Why don't you have a Wall of Fame with a dozen book-quality whitetails in your den? Do you feel the pressure? Are you ready to quit hunting and take up bowling or are you ready to get your game on?

We should get square with each other in this book. We should talk about what it takes to kill big, free-ranging deer every year. Let's not talk around the subject any more. We should figure out – together – why you are NOT doing it already. Did you know that every year, the same few guys, the guys who are committed to taking big deer, ACTUALLY DO IT? Did you know that? And did you know that big deer live in your neighborhood? So, what is your problem?

I am willing to bet that your problem is actually quite simple. You do not believe in yourself. You say you hunt "because it is part of our heritage" or that you "enjoy the wholesome outdoor experience and the ethics of the chase" or how about this one: "Well, any deer taken fairly and legally is a trophy." With all due respect, and at the risk of losing you as a reader right now, I could go out on a limb and say that kind of talk is for losers, but I do not really believe that. In reality, I am just thankful that most people do not believe enough in themselves because that leaves more big deer for me. Counting all the gear, licenses, magazines (and of course the books!) and the BS you take from your spouse, you could buy a hell of a lot of hamburger with the money you spend hunting ... and some fancy toys for your kids, too.

You are probably hunting harder, but not smarter. Although you know better, it has become just too easy to keep on doing what you are doing now. Am I right? Heck, I do not mean to insult you. I absolutely used to be the same way. For years, I hunted from dark to dark every possible day I could get in the woods, and I pretty much took whatever animal came along first. At some point, I got frustrated that I was killing 100-pound does and button bucks every year while other hunters were dragging really big honkers out of the woods.

When I had enough, I decided to take what you might call my "personal hunting inventory" and try to figure out what I was doing wrong. So, while I know exactly how you feel, I am here to tell you that I did not arrive at a hunting strategy by being struck by a bolt of lightning. For nearly 40 years now, I have hunted all over North America, and I have had plenty of help, beginning with my dad, John. I have read a thousand magazine articles, studied countless hours of video and been out there on dozens and dozens of hunting trips. Over the years, my hunting philosophy and the specific strategies I employ to kill big, mature animals every year has evolved. Now, it is time to share it with you, because I know my methods and ideas will work for you as well as they have worked for me.

So, let's get it all written down here and now. By reading this book and applying what you read, you can achieve your highest hunting goals. Let's be frank with one another though. I am assuming that your goal is to kill mature deer every year. Based on my experience, it is not going to be terribly easy to go from complacency to confidence and victory, but is anything that is truly worthwhile ever easy?

Nevertheless, I am totally convinced that if you believe, you can achieve. Even if it isn't easy. It almost sounds un-American, doesn't it, not to be easy. On the other hand, I know that if you read this book and apply the principles we set down here to your own hunting, you can go out there and DO IT. And oh, the feeling you'll experience when you walk up on that first really big mature buck!

"Dear, call the taxidermist."

Tim Hooey
Litchfield, Michigan
January 2004

PREFACE
How To Take Mature Deer Every Year

#1: Recognize that someone is killing mature deer every year. Make this decision: "That someone is going to be me."

#2: Understand that mature deer live within driving distance of your home. Repeat to yourself until you believe: "I am going to find them."

#3: Accept that there is a difference between "trophy hunting" and intent to harvest only mature game animals. Go with intent. It will satisfy you more in the long run.

#4: Be certain that your spouse and hunting buddies understand and support your commitment to take only mature deer. If that happens, it is going to make your efforts easier.

#5: Remind yourself that thinking about something does not make it real. Until you write down your intentions, your commitment to take mature deer every year is meaningless.

#6: Finally, writing something down does not make it happen. Unless you act immediately with sustained enthusiasm on your commitment, you will not succeed.

Chapter 1

In The Beginning

I clearly remember making the commitment that changed the course of my hunting life. It must have been important because it took place about 30 years ago, and it altered my life for the better, permanently.

The first time Tim went hunting, he and his father, John Hooey (left), bagged rabbits and pheasants. Already a trapper, Tim was forever hooked on the outdoor life. A few years later, John bought his son a bow.

On that day, a change in the way I thought, a change in how I imagined myself as a hunter, revolutionized the way I hunt. The decisions I made then changed the results of my hunting and, in a small way (Or maybe not. Who knows how these things are measured?), had a profound effect on my life as well. Here is how it began:

A heavy blanket of frost lay sprinkled over the New Jersey woods. The crinkled, brown leaves beneath it crunched like potato chips as I trudged through the bare trees and brambles toward the stand. When I inhaled, the cold air froze in my throat. When I exhaled, my breath hung before me like some magic vapor. The day was clear and crisp, but at least there was no wind and the silence of the woodlot felt like a living presence.

I got up a little late and so was in a hurry. Careless, I let hot cocoa slosh out of a mug as I was loading stuff into my 1965 slant-six Chevy truck. Cocoa soaked the camo pants and the lightweight long-handles under them. Even after I tried to dry out with a rag from the floorboard, the splotch on my leg was very cold. I turned the heat in the cab to its highest setting, cracked the windows and wondered if deer would smell the cocoa.

My hunting buddies, Bill and John, were waiting at the diner shortly after 5:00 a.m. Experienced bowhunters who were a good dozen or more years my senior, they had a lot of tips and information to share. If I were the least bit careless, they might occasionally share a bit of mischievous misinformation, too. Later, they would laugh and lie about it and maybe offer to buy breakfast if I was sore at them. I was lucky to have these older mentors.

Well, that day I had permission to hunt a nearby farm and had already been out there a couple times just looking around. On the second trip, I nailed some 2 x 4s to the sides of a couple of trees for a stand. They were mostly ends and pieces of board that I had daubed with green and black paint for camouflage. You understand the kind of stand. It was solid until after a few years in all-season weather, when it would become an accident waiting to happen, except that this farmer was adamant that he wanted it down as soon as the season was over.

Anyway, I liked the stand and felt comfortable there. It was the kind of platform that allowed me to move around. At 17, it was still easy to become too bored or too stiff or too cold from standing in one place all morning. From where I parked the truck, it was only a 300- to 400-yard walk.

In those days, New Jersey was not overrun with deer, but deer tracks and deer droppings were scattered all over that farmer's woodlot. The spot looked good enough, and I knew I could take a deer there.

My dad, John Hooey, taught me to hunt deer with a shotgun when

Old-style permanent treestands were state-of-the-art when Tim Hooey began hunting. However, after a couple of years of exposure to the elements 24-7, these stands become dangerous. Good spot, bad stand.

I was just a kid, and as a teenager, I often hunted by myself. I took up bowhunting at the age of 11 when he handed me a Bear Grizzly recurve for Christmas. So, by the time I was 17 years old and meeting Bill and John for breakfast, I thought of myself as an experienced hunter. Big tracks, bucks. Little tracks, does. Be patient, pick a spot and shoot within my ability.

I took whatever deer came along, but it had always been a doe or a small buck. I consoled myself by reassuring mom and dad that they did not taste different than great big deer. Maybe they even tasted better than some old trophy-class wall-hanger.

By the time I made it to the treestand that morning, climbed up onto the platform, took everything out of my pockets, nocked an arrow and leaned the bow against a tree, I was sweating and needed to cool off. I took off my jacket and the hat with the foam insulation from the BoxMart down the road.

I had really built a head of steam walking through the woods that morning. Taking off my clothes instantly felt better. Finally, however, conscience got the better of me and to be on the safe side – apprehensively thinking ahead an hour or so to when I would begin to shiver and need to get down and take a walk or pour a cup of cocoa from the thermos – I put my hat and coat back on.

My feet were cold too. The spilled cocoa on my leg was going to be a problem until I got used to it. The pants and long underwear obviously were not going to dry out. What a morning!

Standing on that narrow, homemade stand, off the ground maybe a whole 12 feet, I yawned and stretched like I was at the beach. It was the first time I had been there in a few days, but nothing had changed.

Because it was daylight and I could not presently see or hear anything in or from any direction except for a couple of persistent chickadees, I relaxed and took a good look around. The sun was just starting to breach the treetops, and the extra warmth it would bring would be a Godsend.

Right then, while I was moving around carelessly on the stand, was when the deer came into view. A buck was following two does. They were moving out of the woodlot in the direction of the road and coming in my direction. Going to cross the road to another field, I figured, although I could not imagine why. When I saw them, they were already less than a hundred yards away.

The buck was a nice 8-pointer, maybe a 125-class Pope & Younger, although we did not pay any attention to the record books in those days (and probably pay too much attention to them now). The does were typical deer in the 2- to 4-year age class: mature, but not overly large. The three deer were fully dressed in their ashen gray, almost black winter coats. They moved away to the right and disappeared in the tangles. Although I willed myself to stay calm, my heart was racing. This was my first encounter with a live trophy buck!

Hunters who are not from "up north" and who cannot picture deciduous woods in the late fall and winter when all the leaves are down may not be able to appreciate how naked I suddenly felt. The stand was only 12 feet in the air. I just knew the deer had seen me shuffling around. On the other hand, maybe they had not.

Then the buck was broadside, not 20 yards away, walking from my right to my left. Like an apparition, he was just "there," having ghosted in without any noise from the brushy swale where I last saw him, and all by himself. I began to shiver as adrenaline pumped into my bloodstream. The bow was behind me leaning against one of the trees. If I so much as exhaled deeply, he would see my breath in the air and flee with his tail up, flag high. If I did not move, he was going to see me in less than a minute anyway and would then blow while he ran away. "Good-bye, good luck!" he would laugh.

I moved my left arm back toward the bow and felt the string. But I could not pick it up or slide it just by holding the string. Leaning back, I ran a hand up toward the bracket. The bow was a four-wheel Bear Whitetail Hunter, the kind everyone bought for a first compound back in the early '70s. I tried hard to keep the movement screened from the buck, which was walking steadily in my direction.

Touching the bracket, I slid my hand just a little farther and felt the limb. I was picking up the 8-pound bow while stretched out at arm's length and 120 degrees, but I was a football player and in great physical condition. The big 8-pointer was broadside now at 12 yards and just below the lip of the small ridge he had been skirting. My gloved fingers closed around the handle and with every ounce of strength, I horsed that bow back to full draw on the biggest buck of my life.

An hour or so later at the Andover diner, my still-shaking hands reached for a third cup of hot coffee as I retold the story to John and Bill.

"I can't believe it. He was right there in front. I was at full draw and … I froze like a stiff at the morgue. My whole body went into a state of shock! It was buck fever and what happened next really blew my mind. After the buck walked away, he went over to the edge of this thicket and rubbed his head and horns all over an overhanging branch, made a scrape and then peed in it. Wow!"

My two friends' sympathetic demeanor turned to envy. Neither of them had witnessed this behavior in all of their 30 years of combined hunting experience. Nonetheless, they felt my teenage anguish about the

The turning point in Tim's hunting life was in taking this little button buck when he was 17 years old.

buck fever. John, who had taken several big bucks with his bow, offered encouragement.

"Best thing you can do," he said, "is to get right back on the horse! Go home and try to imagine you are in the same place and time. Go out back to your practice target and shoot that buck over and over until you're ready. Then get back out there!"

That is just what I did. Full of determination, I headed back over to the farm, to a location more suited to evening movement, this time carrying the new Baker climbing stand that I had bought with my hard-earned trapping money.

As the afternoon progressed, I began sensing that deer were nearby. A few does passed and a little basket-racked 6-point slipped by, but none had offered a good shot or I would have taken them, certainly the buck. It was not long though before a big doe and two little ones came quartering through the hardwoods. They were on a track that would put them in range and just below a steep ridge of hardwoods. Their route across a bench overlooked an open flat that was flooded with acorns. The three deer moved closer and started to feed on the flat below me.

I really wanted that big doe, but one of the smaller deer fed directly in front of my stand. As I watched the doe, my mind drifted and the smaller deer, a button buck, slipped off to my right almost begging me to take the perfect quartering-away shot it offered.

The arrow did not fly perfectly, but it went right about where it ought to have gone. The deer jumped, spun around and ran while I re-played the shot and felt a gratifying wave of emotion. I had kept calm and repressed the shakes. I drew without getting busted and watched the green GameGetter arrow go right into the deer's boiler.

To say that I was excited would be an understatement. The morning that had been an exercise in frustration and adversity had turned into an afternoon of getting it right. I was not a failure. I wanted to be reckoned as an elite woodsman, not a bumbling fool who got buck fever every time he saw antlers, even the tiny antlers of a button buck.

There was a check station at a convenience store down the road, so I put the deer in the back of the truck and headed over there. I had a good season and capped it off with a good shot. Got my hands bloody. Had a little meat for the family dinner table. I certainly felt better than I had that morning.

Back at the house, the first thing I did was run and tell dad. Then I got on the telephone and called John to tell him the great news. "I got a buck! I got a buck!"

"Nice work," John replied. "I'll come right over and take a look."

John soon showed up and dad walked over to him, shook hands and, gesturing with his thumb over the back of his shoulder, said, "He's in the barn."

Entering the barn, John shouted, "Where's he at?"

"Right here," I replied.

Looking up at John's expression did not leave much to the imagination. It was apparent that he had expected to find a more mature buck hanging in the barn. John caught my dad's eye. Winking, and with half a grin, he went over and looked at the little buck and said what a nice shot I made and that even though he wasn't very big, he was going to be darn good eating.

I kind of laughed and said, "Oh, anybody can kill the real big ones, but it takes a heck of a shot to hit the little ones." I said that, but did not really believe it, and suddenly I felt ashamed of taking another little deer.

The animal itself did not shame me because I had made a good shot. I was ashamed that even though I thought of myself as an experienced hunter, even though I had been hunting for almost 8 years, my sights were set so low. I was ashamed of being satisfied to kill such a small animal when bigger ones walked by unscathed. Until I met John, I had been content just to see deer and take any animal that offered a good shot. Apparently, for all the time and money, such puny results made me happy.

At that moment, I was ashamed that I had not grown very much in the years since my dad first let me hunt on my own. I was ashamed because I could tell that John expected more from me than I expected from myself.

I saw the pride and confidence in John's face when he showed people the bucks on the wall of his trophy room. He would point at each of the mounts and talk about them as if they all had a great story to tell. People would always ask him where and how he did it. I remembered the attendant at the check station, how he was friendly when it was my turn, but he did not say much about my little buck and he was not curious about where I was hunting.

At that moment, I vowed to take big deer from then on, but of course, I was young. I did not understand and was not prepared to make the necessary commitment to get it done. Still, at that moment, here is what I understood:

Point #1: Someone is killing big, mature deer every year. That someone might as well be me.

Where The Cookie Crumbles

Afterwards, I processed my deer into little cutlets and made hamburger and sausage. Eventually, I forgot about my vow to only take big deer. That young buck ate well. He just did not eat for very long. Inside a week, the pile of wrapped, frozen venison grew noticeably smaller. The smaller it got, the more I thought about big deer and the less satisfied I felt. I actually got a little depressed about it, maybe a little angry. I began to resent my friend John who always killed good bucks. It was his fault that I felt this way.

But John was decent enough. He was always helpful and encouraging. He didn't act superior or claim to be some great hunter, but I believed there had to be some formula, some secret technique that he wouldn't share with me. Thinking he might know something that I didn't made me mad. I reasoned that more than likely it was a secret spot where he hunted or maybe a special deer lure that he used.

In the deer-hunting seminars Tim Hooey gives, he stresses the element of total personal commitment and the follow-through actions of dedicated scouting and preparation.

Obviously, what was wrong was that I was hunting the wrong place. Sure, I was successful killing deer around home and had seen that nice buck, but I wanted a deer that caused people to walk over and run their fingers over its antlers. Really admire it, not just say nice things to a kid. Looking back on the time, I suppose I was jealous and just could not quite recognize it.

I decided to try to find out where John was hunting. He was not telling me the truth, I reasoned. There just had to be a honey hole out there somewhere, a place with mixed deciduous hardwoods in scattered woodlots and open farmland. Plenty of edge. Plenty of forage for deer except in the hardest winters.

This mental anguish allowed me to blame the hunting area, the distribution of deer and the New Jersey Game and Fish Department for the small deer I was putting in our freezer. In spite of the obvious faults in this line of reasoning, it allowed me to avoid taking personal responsibility for my hunting success ... or lack of hunting success. If I could talk myself into an attitude, well, everything would be out of my control.

For some reason though, this line of reasoning did not make me happy.

The more I chewed on it, the less I liked this "blame somebody else" solution of just finding a better place to hunt, the right place, the secret place that was hiding the big deer. The farms, woods and swamp were pretty much all the same in the area. The distribution of woodlots where deer took shelter, while uneven, seemed random. There was no real reason to believe that a few miles one way or the other would make a difference in the deer I saw.

However, there was still that small knot of anger in my stomach. I just could not get away from that. Moreover, there truly was a counterbalance, a tiny voice whispering that I was responsible. After all, it was my life.

Students of philosophy say that when the pupil is willing, the teacher will come, and right then, I listened to what I was telling myself.

I had learned just so much as a hunter, come just so far ... and then apparently stopped. I knew how to shoot a deer and track it. I knew how to field dress it. I even knew a little about cooking the meat. I knew a little about stuff "out there."

What I began to realize was how little I knew about "interior" stuff such as my "interior dialogue," the things I told myself, the excuses I made. I blamed others, circumstances, equipment and the government for my failure to grow up faster as a hunter and harvest mature animals. I believed or assumed that I would get better naturally, without much thought or effort on my part. Dad said, "Do this," and I did it. The farmer said, "Hunt here," and I hunted there.

At that moment, I took a giant step toward growing up as a hunter and as a man. I began to understand what it meant to take personal responsibility for my time, my actions, my gear and my learning curve.

Then I Grew Up!

I left home for college shortly afterwards to play football (and study, of course). Then, I headed off to Pensacola, Florida, and flew two overseas deployments above the Mediterranean and Atlantic as a United States naval aviator.

As a pilot, my everyday task was to avoid being killed, and I learned to do that through "Attention to Detail." This was a conscious program. It was hammered into us that our first responsibility was to save taxpayer dollars, and only secondary was the responsibility to save our own skins. Our mission was to give the folks back home some high-quality "bang for their bucks" rather than carelessly losing our lives and the multi-million dollar airplanes we flew.

Like the sea, naval aviation could be very unforgiving. My U.S. Marine Corps drill instructor, "Gunny Campos," said, "If one of you puke pilots ever have a brainfart up there and forget where you are, the only thing that'll stink will be whatever's left of you! And it won't be much."

As a footnote, the pilot training program I went through was well thought out and was literally designed to brainwash students. The navy wanted robots, but robots that could think on their feet (or on their seat), make the right decision and follow through as rapidly and automatically as a heartbeat.

Back then, aviation officer candidates were trained by Marine Corp drill instructors. That experience had an immense impact on my life and would influence everything I did from that time forward. I learned discipline, focus and an ego that said there was nothing I could not achieve if I wanted it badly enough.

Eventually, Northwest Airlines hired me to fly commercial airliners, but in all those years, I never lost my love of hunting or lost touch with the lesson that began unfolding for me almost 30 years ago. Even though I may have at times applied the lesson of "taking responsibility" unevenly in my life, when I remember and apply it, it has been of great value to me throughout my travels. Learning to take personal responsibility for my life and my decisions has made me a better hunter, a better pilot and a better human being.

Chapter 2

Making And Understanding Your Commitment

We're going to take the direct route to harvesting mature deer every year. It's my understanding that unless you are one of the very rare natural-born hunters – and there aren't many of those left in North America (I'm certainly not one of them) – or you happen to live smack dab in a real whitetail "honey hole" – and there actually are some of those – you have to Make A Commitment. It's another way of saying you have to accept "personal responsibility" even if it sounds a bit preachy.

Making A Commitment is half easy and half hard; half thinking or deciding and then half doing. Thinking about it has to come before doing anything about it or you're going to botch it. You will get lost in the effort and not understand why you are making so much fuss and trouble. You will ask, "Isn't there an easier way?" and I will ask you right back, "Aren't you taking the easier way now?" Remember, your objective is to drag mature deer out of the woods every year, without fail.

Deciding to Go Forward: Understanding Intentions and Issues

Deer are not scattered evenly across the US and Canada. They are not like molecules of gas that spread to fill a vacuum evenly. Civilization has dramatically altered the natural landscape, but even before the coming of the European and African colonists, deer numbers were irregular on the continent.

Nevertheless, deer live practically everywhere there is something for them to eat and a place for them to sleep undisturbed:

• Suburbanites between New York City and Boston are complaining right this minute about deer destroying their flowerbeds.

Tim believes that hunters often overlook mature deer in their own neighborhood by focusing too much on listings in the record books.

• As far as we know, in spite of the spread of chronic wasting disease, bluetongue and various brain worms, deer have never been as numerous as they are now in the Midwest and the South.

• Along with alligators and trophy mosquitoes, deer abound in the Florida Everglades.

• And you can hunt deer on arid mesas of Arizona and bear-infested islands off the coast of Alaska.

Wherever there are deer, there are mature deer, and that means there are trophy deer. Population dynamics argues that there must be, just to maintain a healthy herd. Sure, some areas of North America produce greater numbers of huge, wall-hanger racks than others. Iowa is arguably better than South Carolina, for instance. Nevertheless, every state and the lower tier of Canadian provinces grow deer that will qualify for the record books: whitetails, mulies, Sitka or Coues deer.

"There are no big deer near where I live" is no longer an acceptable excuse.

Point #2: Mature deer live within driving distance of my home.

Filling the record books – the Boone & Crockett and Pope & Young record keeping systems – is incidental to your purpose, by the way. We are not interested in becoming "trophy hunters." Trophy hunting means leaving home with the intent to kill a deer that fits someone else's definition of a trophy. It is book-bound thinking, and didn't we get enough of that in elementary school? Calling yourself a trophy hunter means you have bought into someone else's system, a confining structure of measurements and duplicate copies and official rules. It's a bit like going to the office.

Freeing yourself from as many artificial rules and regulations as possible is a big part of making a commitment to harvest only mature big-game animals. It is a decision to conform to internal standards rather than the external standards of some private club. Throw out the idea that you cannot harvest a mature deer, a buck or a doe, because it won't make the book. You must also throw out the idea, for example, that having a manicured front yard or being president of the P.T.A. or the Lion's Club are the most important things in life. Once you make a commitment, lots of stuff needs to change.

The only artificial rules and regulations you need to accept are those that define what is legal and others that whisper to us what is ethical and what is not. We abide by the state's laws because they are written to promote the general good of hunters and game populations. Secondly, we have grown up to know the difference between right and wrong. This should be sufficient.

Point #3: There is a difference between "trophy hunting" and intent to harvest only mature game animals.

The objective of your commitment is to need help dragging big deer out of the woods every year.

This is probably as good a time as any to talk about hunting and the care and feeding of our egos. Is making a conscious decision to kill only mature deer an "ego trip?" Yes, I believe that pretty well sums it up.

We are so immersed today in the popular culture of celebrity – Madonna's breasts and Bill Clinton's hair and angry basketball players covered with bizarre tattoos – that we have begun to think of ego as a bad thing. It isn't. Ego is like a handgun. It is neither good nor bad. We have a natural human desire to want people to pat us on the back, but the most important pat on the back is the one we give ourselves. Internally driven personal goals, motivated by consciously thought-out strategies and objectives—not externally driven standards—define a healthy ego trip. That is what makes all the difference.

We all have an ego. Accept that and make the most of it.

Making an ego-commitment to kill only mature animals lets us approach hunting mature deer with an awareness of what we want and who we want to be. Then it lets us make a conscious plan to get from There to Here. That plan becomes our "strategy." Patton and Washington would understand. We make a plan and then act on the plan. Think and decide; then, act and follow through.

Most mature deer are taken in the evening. Finding deer at night will test your tracking skills and sometimes – because it is late, you are tired, you have family and work commitments – it will test your commitment as well.

Now, I said from There to Here and that sounds backwards at first. If we take a trip, we know exactly where we are starting, but only have a vague idea – a memory, a spot on a map, a compass heading – of where we want to go. Strategic whitetail hunting is just the opposite. We start by knowing exactly where we want to end up – taking mature deer – but with only the most obscure idea of where we are beginning. Asking the question, "Why aren't I taking better-quality deer?" proves the point that we are not sure where we are when we begin.

As I have said, there is a difference between trophy hunting and hunting mature, adult deer. It is not hair splitting. The difference is our intent as hunters, and intent is the thinking part of killing deer. The difference is maximizing our potential as human beings and before we get on with the tactical tricks for fooling a deer's natural instincts, this is your first stop. This is the strategic element of deer hunting.

Before he made a commitment to take only mature deer, Tim took this small, 6-point basket-rack buck. "To expand the age structure in and the health of your deer herd," Tim says, "this is the kind of deer you let walk."

Our larger intent as hunters is to maximize our human potential. We look around at the universe and despite the powerful telescopes we point at the heavens and the radio signals we send precariously into the ether, we have not had any luck finding other life, not even a single miniscule microbe. As far as we know, we are part of one very small oasis in a vast, empty and expanding universe. (It probably isn't that way, but that's the way it feels.) So taking the life of a big-game animal, the killing we do on purpose, ought not to be a casual experience.

We want to immerse ourselves completely in the outdoor experience, to become, like recruits hooked by US Army commercials, "All that we can be." Since I had my first, tentative awakening as a teenage hunter, the day I began to understand that "luck" was my own responsibility, I have grown to understand that hunting is one way for me to maximize my potential.

Hunting and flying, plus being a father and husband, are how I eventually want to be remembered. I made that decision consciously, and then I put it down on paper. Usually, by the way, if we actually want our plans to work rather than just be loveable failures, we need to write them down.

Hunting is a means to an end, not an end in itself. It is one means to becoming fully awake, to become completely alive. That is what the Spanish philosopher Ortega y Gasset meant in his famous book, *Meditations on Hunting*, when he summarized that the hunter was the "alert man."

What does it mean to awaken into the 21st century? It isn't a silly question. It is a matter of making informed decisions. We are shielded from millions of years of our own evolution as hunters and scavengers by our technology. Computer simulations shield us from blood on our hands. Paper separates us from sweat on our brow. A pick-up truck separates us from blisters on our feet.

Now, technology is not a good thing. Technology is a great thing. Without it, we would still be cowering from leopards and hyenas on the plains of Africa, scrounging for bugs and roots, gnawing on the bony leftovers after lions and vultures ate their fill. Technology in the form of a 300-fps carbon arrow, for instance, is our great equalizer. Technology is one of the things that define us as humans. But make no mistake. It is not the speed of the arrow that kills the deer. It is our learned, disciplined ability to get close and put the arrow in its vitals that kills it.

Like the trophy books, technology is NOT the end we are seeking as hunters. Technology does not wake us up. Our technology just gives us the tools to proceed. Our intent need not be to reject the high-tech gear that makes our lives easier. We may not like to admit this, but we are too tiny to reject our culture. Imagine a fish rejecting the ocean or a bird its feathers. We push away hunting rifles only to be captivated by single-cam bows. We build our own recurve bows and then shoot sophisticated carbon arrows. We dress in buckskin ... bought from a mail-order catalog. We cannot any more reject the trajectory of a 180-grain bullet from a 30-06 than we can command the tides. Technology gives us the tools to wake up, to make choices with an understanding of the costs and consequences.

To summarize what I'm saying, our intent is to understand with an open mind, to accept with an open heart, and then to jump into a commitment as deep as we need to jump to accomplish our goal. "Intent" isn't something we just dream about. It is a two-part concept: something we decide followed by something we do. It's like making a contract with ourself.

What the technological revolution of the past couple hundred years has brought us is the ability to choose, and choice is the basis of commitment. We choose to raise our standards. We choose to let small deer walk by our stand. We choose to take only mature deer. Because we can, we do.

Just a few thousand years ago, people did not have the range of choices we have. They had to hunt and gather with diligence every day or they would starve. They had to kill the giant cave bear, no matter how afraid they were, or their children would die of exposure. When they speared a big-game animal, or even a little one, they feasted; when they did not, they went hungry.

Making up our mind is the first part of killing big, mature deer every year, but it is an empty gesture unless we write it down and move on to the second part, follow-through.

Decision Time and Implications

Make up your mind to kill only mature deer. You can make this decision right this minute, but you know this first part is easy ... and tricky. If you are dissatisfied with continually taking small deer, the number one step is – Stop! Pass on the infants. Make a decision to take only mature animals and stick with it. Make a conscious decision to do whatever it takes. Tell yourself, "That's it!" You aren't going to take scrawny, immature deer any longer even if, every now and then, it could mean a winter without venison. You aren't going to be content any longer with the scraps from someone else's feast.

Once you have gotten this far, write down your commitment. Here's where the rubber meets the road, where you move from only thinking about it, imagining yourself with a quality animal, to taking action.

Before you go any further though, you have to level with yourself. Do you mean what you have written? Do you really think of it as a binding

Not everyone will take your hunting ambition seriously. Part of the success equation will be a freezer full of venison, some fine racks on the wall and a lot of personal satisfaction!

contract? If you don't, the gesture is worthless. And, what if your spouse sees the note? Or your hunting buddies?

Before someone happens to read your contract, be proactive. Share it with them. In fact, it's a pretty good idea to discuss this change, from simply going out hunting to operating from a hunting strategy, with your significant others. After all, if you are serious, the changes are going to involve them. If you think it won't involve your spouse, what do you think he or she is doing all day Saturday when you are out in a treestand? Twiddling her thumbs? Is he happily babysitting the kids? I doubt it.

After you make up your mind to take home only mature deer, to put 100 pounds of processed venison in the freezer each year rather than half that, you may need to exercise your best negotiating skills to bring your partners on board. If they support you, if your spouse agrees and your hunting buddies go along with it, it is going to make your journey much easier. But be prepared to negotiate.

With your hunting buddies, this could be easy, at least on the surface. You are not committing them to a whole lot except maybe benefiting from your hard work. If you find some dynamic place to hunt, they will go along on the hope that they get to tag a big deer too. Plus, they will be there when you need drag assistance. If your photo is published in the newspaper or in a magazine, they get a vicarious thrill. "I know that guy!" You will be carrying them, and it won't cost them a thing.

If you are serious about making a commitment, your spouse and hunting buddies need to understand that you are serious. There's nothing worse than having someone else screw up your hunt. (It's too easy to do that without any help.) "Oh, sorry about that! I wasn't thinking," simply won't cut it where you are going. Your friends must understand about no smoking or chewing tobacco in your truck, ever; or that if they get a day off in the middle of the week, they cannot run out and climb up in your hunting stand. They need to know, maybe over a beer (that you provide), that it is not "business as usual" with you any longer. You are separating from your former self. Barring an emergency, there won't be any more getting to the hunting area late and climbing into a tree after the sun is up. But remember that it isn't about them. It's about you.

Point #4: If my spouse and hunting buddies understand and accept my commitment to take only mature deer, it's going to make my efforts easier.

Your spouse will have her or his own agenda and your hunting buddies will have their own reasons for hunting with you. Most of your friends are, let's be honest, happy to harvest any deer, especially if they are bowhunting. For most guys, trying to take a wild animal home to eat is a diversion. It is something they do when the weather is good and when there's not a kid's hockey game or when their favorite football team isn't on television. You used to be like that, but once you make a conscious commitment, once you write it down and discuss it with your significant others (your family and your hunting buddies), you graduate to a different league. Your decision separates you from the average guy in the woods and you have become a "serious hunter."

Be prepared for two kinds of response. First, not everyone will take you seriously. Second, some may even think it is comical, laughing behind your back (of course). The idea of showing them a written contract with yourself will seem "nerdy." You have to focus on the fact that the racks on your wall and the extra pile of venison burgers at your cookouts will eventually be the proof that you have changed. When they see your first big deer, they

Is this fine buck a trophy-book buck or an excellent mature deer that makes you very proud of putting yourself in the right place and making a great shot? The difference is your intention. "Interior motivation is healthier and more important in the long run than external motivation," Tim says.

will want to change too, but – and you will realize it by then – wanting to and doing it are two entirely different things.

Even though they won't do it consciously, your hunting buddies may even sabotage your efforts. Cut them some slack. They are used to the old you, the "Yeah, we're a little late, but what the heck." you. If your buddies resist, you will have to either cajole them or hunt less frequently with them. Your success may be a little threatening, so you have to convince them that your decision is strictly personal. After you prove that there's a new you in the woods – and there will be – prepare for some small displays of jealousy. Don't be offended. It's natural, and it's not about you.

Now, if your spouse resists the fact that you will need his or her support and that you will be spending more time both getting ready and hunting,

Making a contract with yourself is a life-altering event. It is important that you do not cut corners in pursuing success. A full-body safety and hunting harness is immensely important for your confidence, for your safety and, ultimately, for your hunting success.

you've got your hands full. Be prepared to compromise. Never compromise on your hunting goal, but find other areas where you can be flexible without resentment. The hunting mission has to be, if not Number One in your life, right up there, and your spouse may not like that. It's understandable. Your husband or wife will not object to your goal so much as to its consequences, its spin-offs; their life will change in large or small ways because of your commitment. Be gentle. Be accommodating. But know where to draw the line.

So, when you are not preparing or reading or scouting or hunting, you will, for example, have to pitch in more to fix meals for the family, play with the children and wash your spouse's car. Gas it up and get it detailed every now and then. Be sure your partner knows that they are a full and necessary part of your new hunting equation … and your life.

If you can't make this work with your spouse and your hunting buddies, you are going to have trouble making your commitment stick. It won't be impossible; it just won't be easy. Be prepared to do what is necessary to make your dream come alive.

Point #5: Thinking about it doesn't make something real. Until I write down my intentions, my commitment to take mature deer every year is meaningless.

Chapter 3

The Paperwork

For readers who thought I was kidding about writing out a contract, I offer the following example. We know that contracts are full of "whereas" and "the party of the first part" and "therefore." A contract is designed to reduce what is commonly called wiggle room, although it certainly does not eliminate it. Do not for one minute think that you can skip this part and still be successful. The contract is the binder, a little part of conscience that you put down on paper as a thorny stimulus when you get tired or lazy.

This contract is a little different, however. It is a contract that you make with yourself. The more you think it through and discuss it with your family and your hunting buddies, the more difficult it will be to sleep in on dreary mornings. The more people watching you, the harder it is to slide by and take a substandard deer. That in itself is a damn good reason to let people know what you are doing. It helps keep you honest. You might even go so far as to have it witnessed by a couple friends and notarized, then hung on the wall above your workbench. Every office supply store sells certificate paper that will make this look good. If it quacks, it's a duck. If it looks good, it will be good. If you think you don't need it, try to remember how many New Year's resolutions you have kept.

Regardless of how many others you involve in the commitment equation, the pressure you put on yourself ought to be sufficient to force you to live up to the contract. After all, we are preaching internal motivation and the adherence to standards that YOU set because they are right for YOU, not the standards other people may devise, even other people you respect. We are talking about consciously addressing the problems that keep you from maximizing your human hunting potential and taking advantage of your bountiful opportunities.

So, keeping it simple, here is a sample:

CONTRACT

Whereas I _____ (print name) have been hunting for _____ (number) years and have rarely taken a mature deer.

Whereas I am dissatisfied with harvesting small, immature deer.

Whereas I have made a conscious decision to maximize my potential as a hunter.

I therefore make a **Commitment** *to harvest only mature deer.*

In Recognition of the discipline required to successfully proceed with this Commitment, I request all friends, family and interested parties render aid and encouragement to help me remain dedicated to that goal.

I will prepare. I will hunt legally and ethically. On easy days and on difficult days, I will do my best. Until I, in full awareness of my actions, choose to make this contract null and void, I will not harvest an immature deer, but I will respect all game animals and I will succeed.

_____
(Your Signature)   *(Date)*

_____ *(Witness)*   _____ *(Witness)*
_____ *(Date)*   _____ *(Date)*

Chapter 4

Understanding Deer

Whitetail deer are the most abundant and widespread deer species in North America. The species (*Odocoelius virginianus* for those with a scientific need to know) numbers upwards of 25 million animals within the continental US, reportedly about the same number as in 1492, the year Christopher Columbus "discovered" the New World.

Bringing home big, mature deer (such as this one that Tim and Lou Haubner are posing with from their River Ridge Ohio property) every year is an achievable challenge, says master bowhunter Tim Hooey (right). Researchers such as Dr. Karl Miller of the University of Georgia agree that there are as many deer in the US and Canada now as there were when Columbus first landed in the New World.

These deer thrive because they adapt to practically every ecological niche. As we have previously mentioned, whitetails are currently found in almost every neighborhood in the US, probably not too far from where you live.

No other species of big-game animal has drawn such a mass following as the whitetail. People get downright giddy about deer, and they certainly evoke a passion among outdoor folks. Their antlers are things of great beauty, and calendars that feature glossy photos of deer sell like crazy. Whitetails have become the primary outdoor topic for outdoor books, magazine articles, videos and television series.

If you are going to become proficient at killing mature whitetails, you must first understand them. Deer are like hunters. The longer they live, the more they learn. To hunt mature deer, you need to understand how a mature deer's behavior is different from that of a young deer.

A Brief History

Pioneers and Native Americans were dependent for survival on what they could grow or kill. East of the Mississippi River, white-tailed deer were a significant portion of their diet.

Early, white, market hunters viewed the whitetail as an inexhaustible source of food, and by the late 1700s, deer were scarce near the thickly settled portions of America. No fish or game laws had been written then, and deer were shot for the table or campfire in every season, day and night. The growing settlements, stretching well across the Appalachian Mountains by 1800, simply had no respect for wildlife habitat. Predictably, the result was extreme over-harvesting.

In the 350 years from the initial European settlement to the awakening of an outdoor consciousness, many animal species came close to extinction. By the early 1900s, it is reliably estimated that the whitetail herd in North America had been reduced from 25 million to less than one million animals and perhaps to as few as half-a-million, an astonishing 98 percent reduction.

In the 20th century, courageous hunters and outdoorsmen were at last able to push forward a conservation agenda that pulled game species back from the brink. These men established fish and game departments, regulated seasons, harvest quotas and preserves. All that time, the whitetail deer hung on and adapted. As a result of regulating the pressure, by mid-way into the 1900s, whitetails were on the comeback trail along with the wild turkey, elk, pronghorn antelope and other popular game species.

By the early 1900s, scientific studies began to reveal the intricacies of deer biology. Passage of the US Pittman-Robertson Act in 1937 finally channeled sportsman's dollars into wildlife research, active management programs and hunter education. As a result, the pace of study increased.

Although the whitetail suffered because of the expanding human population, there were some spin-off consequences. In 1996, noted deer biologist James Kroll called attention to what he believes is a form of "unnatural selection" that resulted from the decimation of the deer herd in North America, essentially prior to the 1900s. "Deer escaping harvest were those who did not behave in normal whitetail fashion. They were more secretive, more nocturnal, and more flighty than their ancestors. The result is an animal much more difficult to kill."

Citing anecdotal evidence (observational, but not the least bit scientific) from the wide-open and rarely hunted King Ranch in Texas, Kroll suggests that even mature whitetails will allow hunters to approach within 40 yards because that particular "flight distance" is the distance needed to avoid close shots by aboriginal hunters. Outside 40 yards, Kroll said, deer do not spook if your approach is casual. Once you cross that imaginary boundary, however, they flee. He believed this was primarily due to the limited-distance weapons man used to hunt them for thousands of years. Still, that cannot be a complete explanation.

Man has been on the earth for several million years as an identifiable species, but only 40,000 or so years as *Homo sapiens*. Until fairly recently in our evolution, we have been a minority actor in the life and death struggle that defines eating and being eaten and the evolution of species on earth. Apparently designed to be a source of protein for carnivores, to convert one kind of energy into another (sunlight and browse into flesh and protein), deer have been killed and eaten by every type of wild creature that eats meat in North America: wild dogs, cats, bears and maybe even alligators and eagles. I believe a deer's 40-yard flight distance is more a learned response to the lunge of a jaguar or the final sprint of a pack of wild dogs rather than creeping human hunters armed with poison-tipped spears and arrows.

Modern hunting technology and methods (i.e., firearms) have forced deer to become an even more elusive animal, one that is able to "adjust quickly to any unnatural occurrence." So, Kroll thinks we humans have forced deer to adapt, to change their behavior or end up on our dinner plate. However it has happened, that is the equation we face today, a naturally elusive animal that adjusts rapidly to unnatural or threatening circumstances. You could say whitetails are extremely smart animals.

Physical Characteristics

The whitetail is named for its most distinctive feature, the large white flag we see so often waving from its rear end. That white flag is not a signal for surrender, but rather means, "See ya! I'm outta here."

The rest of a deer is brown except for little spots around its big brown eyes, right? Not so fast, Bambi. The color of a deer's coat changes with the season, from a bright, rusty red in the summer to a deep gray in the midst of a cold, snowy winter. Their underside is white and deer have a white patch on their throat and around their eyes.

Twice a year, a deer will shed its coat. Hair by hair, it changes both color and thickness of its coat, which is thicker and longer in winter and thinner and shorter in summer.

Born in late spring or summer, a fawn's coat is similar to an adult's, but it has a multitude of white spots that only disappear at 4 to 5 months. Typically, by early November, male fawns weigh around 85 pounds. Females are about 10 pounds lighter. That first year, as young bucks become yearlings, they gain to an average of 150 pounds. At any time of their comparable life span, does are 20 percent lighter than bucks of the same age set. A mature buck can weigh more than 250 pounds and freaky deer weighing more than 400 pounds have been hauled into check stations.

Now, we can talk hair color and the texture of deer toenails for hours, but the engrossing detail that makes whitetails so fascinating is their antlers. Let's face it. If it weren't for their antlers, deer would be just another wild bovine, too difficult to domesticate and, therefore, of limited social value.

A buck fawn has bumps on his skull where antlers will grow when he is older. One-and-a-half-year-old bucks may have from one to six points on each antler. Based on a study of more than 2000 deer checked during the 1990 season, the Nebraska DNR concluded that the average young buck was a 3 x 3. About 20 percent were 4 x 4s.

The places we each hunt near our homes will vary from this study. Nebraska certainly is not typical of traditional whitetail habitat. In many places I have hunted, Michigan and Pennsylvania and New Jersey and Wisconsin, for instance, there are great numbers of deer, but there are great numbers of hunters, too. This makes it difficult for bucks to attain substantial antler growth or even the age necessary to grow big antlers. It doesn't mean big deer are not present in heavily hunted areas; they are. It just means that the survivors have learned that pressure from humans is deadly, and they have become extremely elusive. To kill them, you will have to make a Commitment and ramp up your skills.

Dr. Karl Miller has built a reputation on his wildlife dynamics research with white-tailed deer at the University of Georgia. Not long ago, Tim had an opportunity to ask him about some of the pressing questions that face hunters in the field every day. Excerpts from this conversation appear throughout this book as sidebars to the text. In this installment, Tim asks about deer tracks and what we can learn from them.

Deer Tracks

Tim: Can you tell the sex of a deer by the track it leaves?

Dr. Karl Miller: The only way to positively identify the sex of a deer from the track it makes is to find the track with the deer still in it. Otherwise, numerous studies have found that while there are some sex-related variations in tracks, the overlap in the tracks is too large to allow accurate predictions.

Deer hooves are essentially fingernail material and the amount of contact they make with the ground compared to the deer's size is amazingly small. You could put all of a 200-pound deer's hooves inside the footprint of a 200-pound hunter. This small hoof size plus a healthy deer's amazing natural strength and the special "springing ligament" that stretches to the hoof, gives the deer terrific sprinting speed and the ability to make quick changes in direction. Hooves grow all the time, about 2-1/2 inches a year.

While no researcher can give you a foolproof system for distinguishing between bucks and does strictly from their tracks, here are some general observations of my own:

• Hunters correctly observe that large tracks are usually bucks, but in average-size tracks, there is no way to tell between bucks and does.

• A mature buck's hooves tend to be more rounded at the tip than do does, particularly the front hooves, but terrain and soil conditions are a factor here also.

• The presence or absence of dewclaw impressions depends on a variety of factors and is not a reliable indicator of sex.

• Small tracks accompanying a larger track suggest a doe with a fawn.

• Hunting in the snow has some advantages. Because bucks and does urinate differently, a urine trail in the snow – as opposed to a spot which could be made by a doe or a young buck – is a pretty good sign of a buck. Bucks often urinate as they walk. Also, two tracks close together with urine splashed around them probably indicate that the deer rub-urinated and that is more of a buck behavior than that of a doe. Finally, there is a tendency for bucks to leave drag marks with its front feet in a light snow.

According to professional deer biologists like Dr. Karl Miller of the University of Georgia, there are only two ways to accurately tell the sex of a deer by looking at the track: make a lucky guess or see the track with the deer standing in it.

Deer Nutrition

Aside from basic biology, that is to say the deer's genetic inheritance, nutrition plays the most significant role in the development and maintenance of a healthy body weight and a buck's antler structure. Nutrients are processed in a whitetail's four-chamber stomach:

• The first chamber is called the rumen. It is the largest of the four stomach-sacs and stores partially chewed and digested food. It allows a deer to eat more than it can immediately digest. Thus, it can eat all night and digest the food while lying in its bed all day. From the rumen, a deer regurgitates some of its quickly eaten browse for additional chewing and digestion by salivary enzymes.

• Chamber two is the reticulum. It shares the responsibility with the rumen for turning raw, partially digested food into energy and is a transitional stomach for the final two sacs.

• Exiting the reticulum, undigested food and waste continues into chamber three, the omasum, where it is further broken down and finally passed to chamber four, the abomasum.

When was this rub made and why was it made in this location? Learning as much as possible about deer physiology and behavior is a giant step to becoming, to paraphrase Spanish philosopher Ortega y Gasset, the alert and aware hunter.

Complete food digestion takes from 2 hours to 6 days, depending on the type of food. For instance, sweet corn is easier to digest than willow bark. For fawns, the stomachs are fully developed at 12 weeks, right about the time of weaning.

A whitetail's diet should include plenty of the same stuff you and I eat: protein, carbohydrates, sugars, fats, minerals and vitamins. According to studies from Kansas and Iowa, places where huge amounts of corn are grown commercially, it can constitute up to half of a deer's diet from planting until harvest. Although deer are commonly observed in alfalfa fields, this crop is a relatively minor food source. Clover is a draw and sweet peas are like ice cream sundaes.

Native foods constitute half or more of what most deer eat. Examples include woody vegetation, particularly buck brush and wild rose with lesser amounts of honeysuckle, dogwood, chokecherry, plum, red cedar, pine and a host of other things. Forbs, particularly sunflowers, are important, while grasses and sedges are used seasonally in spring and fall, the difficult times for critters who make their living in the outdoors because these are the in-between times when food sources change.

If you understand the role that seasonal foods play in the whitetail's daily round of bedding and eating and traveling, you can apply the same principles to scouting for mule deer and other big game.

Although whitetails can certainly exist entirely on native foods, they have apparently developed a preference for some farm crops. Perhaps it is because fields are wide open (it is easier for deer to watch for predators) and food is highly concentrated.

Crop damage by whitetails constitutes a significant management problem in big agricultural states. Deer numbers have to be balanced between hunters who typically want "more" game to hunt (usually understood as larger and easier to kill) and traditional chemical-based farmers who would be just as happy with deer simply on postcards. Once big landowners realize they can charge hunters for the use of their property, however, that farm voice quickly changes from protection of their livelihood to enhancement of the wildlife resource. The underlying transactional message is always cash.

Most authorities agree that while nutrition is important to the general health and development of mature deer, it is especially important to fawn survival. Fawns are born in the spring and summer and sufficient food with good nutritional value allows them to begin laying on fat for winter.

Obviously, nutrition plays a large part in antler growth. When a buck is unable to consume the necessary amounts of high-quality forage, antler growth is minimized. According to Kroll, deer researchers at Mississippi State University purchased a 9-year-old buck that had been fed a low-protein, corn-only diet. It had a very small, very thin 4 x 4 rack with a narrow 17-inch inside spread. Fed a 16-percent-protein diet, its next year's rack flourished with 21 points and a 27-inch inside spread!

Genetics and diet rule.

Social Groups

Before their breeding season, adult whitetails live in groups with other deer of the same sex. The female social unit will contain several generations of daughters who have shared the same core area throughout their life. The oldest doe usually assumes the lead, becoming the "alpha female" in this unit.

Young, antlerless bucks, commonly called "button bucks," are included in the doe grouping prior to breeding season. As the rut comes nearer, antlerless bucks are driven out of their home (female) group and sometimes even from their home range altogether. In theory, this prevents inbreeding and inferior breeding, and in this way, deer establish a natural hierarchy that maximizes the reproductive ability of the herd.

Bucks travel in exclusive social units called "bachelor groups" prior to the breeding season. Inside these units, the bucks are aggressive with one another. Like on any public school playground, this establishes a dominance hierarchy based on physical size and strength, antler size, experience, fighting ability and the deer's individual temperament. The result of this aggressiveness is that some bucks breed more than others, and their genetic materials are passed on to future generations in greater abundance.

This dominance hierarchy is a fluid structure for the homeboys. It will change for example when a roaming buck shows up. Perhaps the roamer

When the family understands and supports your passion and commitment as a deer hunter, many of the objections to the time, effort and money you spend will diminish. Pictured right-to-left are Tim's dad, John Hooey, his son Sean and nephew Kevin.

has been kicked out of its own home range by a larger, more aggressive deer; or there has been too much human interference, and it must find another playground. Rank changes also occur as a result of death and disease. It also appears that occasionally a deer will just have a bad day and wake up with a mean streak. Perhaps it indulged in too much wild grape the evening before and picks on all the inferior bucks it can reach. It can all change the next day, but once a hierarchy is established, only the death of dominant participants changes it fundamentally.

Unlike a pack of primates or wild dogs, deer social structure is more fluid. A mountain gorilla band or a wolf pack consisting of males, females and infants lives and forages together permanently through every season. The dominant male can retain his status for years. This is not the situation with deer, which are prey animals and have no strongly cohesive pack or family structure. The dominance hierarchy in a widespread deer herd is subject to change occasionally during the year.

Curiously, just having a big rack or a big, muscular body does not insure that a buck will be the dominant male. Like the playground bully, smaller and more aggressive deer are occasionally known to dominate larger deer. Apparently, this dominance is in part based on what we would call "a bad attitude" if it were displayed in our own peer group.

During the 1999 archery season, I bowhunted in Pike County, Illinois, with outdoor writer Darrin Bradley. He and I were hunting a specific deer, a mature 8-pointer with incredible mass. Bradley claimed that the bases of the 8-point's beams were almost as big around as a soda pop can. I guessed the animal would have made the Boone and Crockett (B&C) record book easily, and that means it was huge, because not one of the top 100 bucks listed in B&C is an 8-pointer. This buck was definitely a world-class individual.

Each evening, we glimpsed this monster 8-point walk into an agricultural river bottom to browse on cut corn and clover. The guy always seemed to be one step ahead of us by staying well out of bow range.

Around the second week in October, the buck simply vanished. We never knew what happened to it, whether it was shot by another hunter or simply wandered away to look for a new home range.

We could see the social-rank-adjustment process began immediately in the deer herd. Surprisingly, when the process began to sort out, a relatively small 100-class buck began entering the fields along the river bottom. This buck strutted and snorted like he owned the place. This animal was so testosterone-driven that he rarely slowed down to put his muzzle in the grass. From the time that little buck entered the field until well past dark, he was chasing and fighting any animal he could reach. Fawns, does, mature bucks … it didn't matter to him.

One particular evening, I saw our 100-class hero throw a much larger, trophy buck to the ground.

That tough little buck hissed, snorted and pawed the ground beneath it continually. It was apparently carving out a niche for itself as the dominant buck in the herd, dominant over bucks that had 40 to 60 more inches of antler and outweighed him by as many pounds! Neither Bradley nor I was excited about this feisty but smallish buck servicing the majority of the does during the rut. So, when it eventually drifted within bow range, I arrowed it on video and then discussed the episode during a regular segment of my television show, *North American Fish & Game*.

This episode illustrates how individual deer can have what we think of as personalities. Deer differ in other, more obvious ways, too. Bucks and does vary in size, shape, growth and metabolic rates, food and cover preference and most other aspects of physiology and biochemistry. Cover and even bedding preferences result from the instinctual motivation of each sex. Bucks tend to stay closer to dense cover while does are not as selective, except when they have young fawns. Does choose a habitat that is most conducive for bearing offspring, preferring cover with accessibility to diversified food selections and season-appropriate thickets for hiding fawns. (It is curious then when a newborn fawn is discovered nestled in the corner of someone's back porch!) Bucks choose habitat where nutritional resources are excellent and favor dense cover as they tend to be more squirrelly about running into strangers, even strange deer, the closer they get to the rut.

The Breeding Cycle

After several months of sexual segregation during fawn-rearing months, whitetails begin to intermingle in late summer and early autumn. Bachelor groups and the big groups of does split apart. This time period alters deer travel patterns as food sources change, and it brings about the most interesting aspect of a whitetail's life cycle.

In these hot months, a buck's velvet-covered antlers reach their full size and then, as the daylight lessens, they begin to harden. Older, mature bucks are usually the first to shed antler velvet. In northern states, bucks complete this task by late August. It isn't completed until late September in the south.

Rising levels of testosterone in a buck's bloodstream trigger "mineralization" or hardening of the antlers. In other words, the more robust the animal, the quicker the process occurs. Bucks that don't produce the necessary testosterone levels, due to an injury to their testicles or perhaps to sickness, may not shed velvet.

With good health and good nutrition, whitetails are prolific breeders. One study of 600 does indicated that about 60 percent bred as fawns, about 6 months old, and virtually all of the older females produced young. A portion of the buck fawns is capable of reproducing, too. Breeding begins in mid-October and peaks in mid-to-late November for adults and about one month later for fawns.

Neither bucks nor does are bound to a single partner. A buck will mate with several does if circumstances permit. In penned conditions, a single buck has recorded as many as 20 successful copulations.

Fawns are born after a gestation period of about 201 days, from early May through late September, with about 60 percent born in June. Does bred when they are less than a year of age normally give birth to a single fawn, but about 10 percent of them give birth to twins. Two-thirds of older does have twins, 21 percent have single fawns and 12 percent have triplets. Therefore, you can expect that 100 fertile does will produce about 191 fawns!

One conclusion to the above statistics is that if deer herds are left unchecked, have sufficient food and good weather, they can practically double in size every year. It's an astonishing concept.

The whitetail's reproductive rate is high compared to, for example, that of the mule deer. Mulies produce approximately 94 fawns per 100 does per year and only 7 percent of females breed as fawns. Compared to 94 percent of whitetails, only 68 percent of mule deer does become pregnant as yearlings. About 79 percent of pregnant whitetail does carry twins or triplets while only 52 percent of pregnant mule deer does have multiple fetuses. It's no wonder the numbers of mule deer are declining while whitetails are extending their range.

At birth, a female whitetail fawn weighs about 5-1/2 pounds and males are a couple pounds heavier. Shortly following its birth, a fawn is capable of standing and walking, but for the first few days its movement is limited. When the fawn is 2 or 3 weeks old, it begins eating vegetation in addition to nursing. Fawns are normally weaned when they are about 4 months old, but they are capable of surviving without milk at 3 months or even younger. Because of predation or some natural weakness or accident, about a third of the fawns do not survive until fall.

Young deer usually establish a home range coterminous with their mother's. While yearling females continue to reside in that area, bucks do not. At about 6 months, their mothers aggressively confront the little bucks, apparently in an attempt to encourage dispersal. Initially, the aggressive advances manifest themselves in body posture and visual contact. If the young buck does not leave as a result of these less aggressive mannerisms, physical attacks are sure to follow. As a result, about 80 percent of all yearling bucks wander off and end up in an entirely different area. We don't know what deer think about this behavior and its causes, but the biological objective may be to prevent inbreeding.

Once deer bachelor groups break up and does begin to drive away their fawns, deer become more receptive to calling. Tim keeps a call tube handy all the time. "Just in case," he says.

Antler Development

Genetics plays a major role in antler development. Although life span and nutrition are certainly important, bucks need to inherit the right genes to achieve maximum antler growth. It is currently believed that inherited genetics patterns determine the configuration of a buck's rack and set the outside parameters for growth in ideal conditions. That said, the quality of available food and factors such as accidents or an inherited sickness have a great influence on length and thickness of the tines and a rack's overall mass.

The first year Tim managed property in Michigan, he culled a few of the deer that did not carry the genetic material to produce wide-racked mature bucks.

Deer in specific areas carry a general rack shape or unique characteristic due to the genetics of the particular "family" of deer that lives there. In Ohio, Michigan and Illinois, racks possess multiple points, tall tines and impressive width. Antlers from Alabama and Florida and Mississippi are usually not as wide or as heavy in mass, but can commonly be very tall. Generally, Texas racks seem to be darker in pigment, wide and tall, but lacking in mass.

A low buck-to-doe ratio offers dominant bucks the opportunity to breed with more does, which in turn produces higher-quality racks. When buck-to-doe ratios are disproportionally skewed, for instance when too many does have been allowed to remain in the herd, dominant bucks are unable to service a high number of does. This means inferior bucks copulate with more does and that eventually produces low-quality racks.

Whitetails establish dominance and superiority in determining a range of deer goodies such as which ones obtain access to the best food, cover, bedding sites, fawn-raising spaces and breeding opportunities. Dominance is established through physical confrontation on a regular basis. True aggression, however, is rare. A puncture from a single antler tine or a sliced eyeball from a doe's sharp front hoof can be deadly. Threats and displays of aggression without physical contact are practiced most often.

Students of whitetail behavior believe that while sparring is primarily used to determine dominance, sparring may not always provide a decisive outcome. Deer spar to determine their opponent's antler configuration as well as to learn about the opposing buck's fighting skills. More often, I think, when bucks spar in a non-decisive manner, they are doing it for fun, for social interaction and recreation. Any experienced hunter can testify to watching deer, especially yearlings, run and play for entertainment, and in late summer, bucks often seem to spar just for fun. Sometimes – just like on the school playground – this recreational sparring can turn into an aggressive battle depending on the temperament of the animals. True fights between bucks usually occur only between relatively evenly matched animals during the rut.

Does engage in both recreational and dominance determination battles although they are more apt to battle over food and fawn-rearing cover. Female deer may begin a battle with direct eye contact, aggressive body language or posture. If dominance cannot be determined by a less aggressive mode, a fight can ensue. Does rise on their hind feet to an upright position and slash like prizefighters. This vicious hoof slapping of mature does can be painful, because their toes are sharp and their legs are very strong, in spite of the fact that they look skinny and bony.

In 1992, a member of a hunting party I am familiar with arrowed a

In his conversation with Dr. Karl Miller, a well-known white-tailed deer researcher at the University of Georgia, Tim asked him about what scientists currently know about deer antlers.

Antlers

Tim: What fascinates us about deer, of course, are their antlers and the fact that they are the primary big-game species east of the Rocky Mountains. Can you give us some insight into the "antler thing?"

Dr. Miller: Well, antlers on deer and caribou and elk are bone, not the hair-like horns we see on pronghorns and goats and sheep or even on Cape buffalo. And antlers grow from their tips, not their base like horns. Nevertheless, all of this headgear is used for scent marking, competition and dominance display.

Antlers begin to grow in late spring, as days get longer. During the summer, they may grow a quarter of an inch in length a day. At this time, they are covered with what we call velvet, a living sheath filled with blood and the essential nutrients – primarily calcium and phosphorous – needed to make bone. Velvet-covered antlers are fragile and sensitive, so bucks are careful not to damage them.

Researchers have identified a "trophic memory center" in the brain of deer. This is what causes a deer to maintain the same general antler configuration from year to year. Normally, if an antler is damaged during growth, the next year's antlers will revert to the basic shape. In deer, however, it is extremely curious and not well understood that some injuries are "remembered" and subsequent antler shape may reflect this abnormality.

By August, antler growth is basically complete and increasing levels of testosterone are found in the buck's system. Whether it is a spike or an atypical monster, the growth has taken about 100 days. All that is left is to shed the velvet, allow the antlers to harden and then use them in competition for females. In a mature buck, shedding velvet may only take a couple hours and big deer usually shed before smaller ones.

Once the velvet is shed, the antler gradually hardens, although it maintains a spongy core in the center, and living tissue connects the antler to the deer's head.

After the rut – from January through March – antlers are cast off. Bucks we have observed always react in what looks like surprise when their antlers fall off. One day you couldn't knock them off with a hammer, and the next, they are lying on the ground. Within about a week, the bone base where the antlers attach scabs over and heals.

In our captive deer herd in Georgia, we notice that larger, dominant deer shed first, but this process varies markedly from one area of the country to another.

Tim: Well, that is all fun and complex, too.

Dr. Miller: Yes, it is. Of course, if you find shed antlers, you know the deer made it through the hunting season and that it will probably be alive the next hunting season … and bigger than before.

mature doe. The party assisted the successful shooter in tracking the animal. Upon discovering the whereabouts of the wounded doe, this fellow decided, against the advice of his friends, that he would save his expensive hunting arrows and finish the harvest manually, with a hunting knife. That contest ended quickly with the hunter suffering numerous bruises and lacerations that sent him to the doctor's office. Although I did not witness the event, I will assure you that this fine fellow will refrain from ever attempting this feat again.

The Sport and Its Management

Each year, more than 15 million people in the US and Canada hunt whitetails. On a personal level, deer hunting is enjoyed as a recreational activity. On a public level, the 21st century is witnessing the conversion of deer hunting to big business at every level. This is a mixed blessing, and I do not believe that in the long run it will be good for the average hunter. On the one hand, deer hunters can look forward to having state-of-the-art equipment coming onto the market rapidly. On the other hand, I believe that access to prime land is going to become a serious problem. While not many years ago we could hunt anywhere free, expensive hunting leases are going to become more customary.

Hunting generates more revenue across the board than any other sport in North America including baseball, football, hockey or basketball. For our whitetail herd to continue to meet our expectations, sportsmen have to organize and support the set-aside of land for hunting, public and hunter education and strong conservation and wildlife management practices. Ducks Unlimited and the National Wild Turkey Federation have gone down this road already for their respective species and each has done a fine job.

Deer management programs are beginning to be implemented by private landowners as well as state departments of natural resources. It was once thought that archers were a relatively insignificant part of these programs, not important in controlling overpopulation problems, but the management program at Clinton Lake, Illinois, disproves this. The Clinton Lake program mandates that hunters harvest a doe prior to tagging an antlered buck. This practice has reduced the area's overpopulation problems, which resulted in endemic herd diseases and high fawn mortality caused, I believe, by fawns born from inferior buck-doe couplings.

It doesn't take a rocket scientist to implement a deer management program. It just takes some commitment and some public support. The essential part? When in doubt, kill does.

Properly administered and protected, a deer management plan can turn an average-to-poor hunting area into buck heaven within a few years.

Some state departments of game and fish such as those in Illinois, Michigan, Iowa, Minnesota and Ohio have implemented large-scale deer-management programs designed to promote quality-buck production. These programs, with weapon mandates such as "shotgun only" and tag lotteries, have been very effective in herd management.

Other states are less focused on overall herd management and instead aim to promote trophy bucks. Missouri currently offers a second 4-day firearm season after the initial 11-day firearm hunt. Occurring in January, the second, late-season hunt has a doe-only harvest objective. I believe the problem with this ill-conceived management plan is two-fold. First, bucks that have already shed antlers are being legally harvested as does. The second season takes place almost 2 months late and all the while the herd has been raping the countryside of available foods. If the second season were scheduled earlier, surviving members of the herd would have more food available over the winter.

According to the Nebraska DNR, deer hunters spent about $1.5 million for hunting permits there in 1990. The amount spent on whitetail hunting and "associated activities" in that state alone was estimated at more than $10 million annually.

I traveled to the Diamond K Ranch in December 1999 to hunt the Texas rut. The 2800-acre working ranch is prime whitetail habitat and is enclosed by the standard, 8-foot fencing that encloses millions of acres of the Lone Star state. Management staff at the ranch says the fence is not so much to keep their whitetails in, as it is to keep inferior whitetails out! The Diamond K strives to use high-protein food sources coupled with a dynamic deer management – and by that I mean doe reduction – program to produce quality racks.

On that hunt, I positioned myself high in a white oak, overlooking a dirt road. The site was bordered by a bushy sendero, which is Spanish for a kind of wide ditch or gully.

Halfway through the hunt, I saw something moving in the brush, so I picked up my binoculars and identified a great set of antlers. I couldn't see the deer's body right away, but it seemed to just be sauntering casually along, and I figured it was my job to put a stop to that.

Many people believe that bowhunting Texas requires supreme stealth. After all, the wide-open terrain resounds to the scuffle of your boots like a church sanctuary to a kid stealing from the collection plate. It amplifies the slightest unnatural sound many times.

I keep a grunt call hanging from a lanyard around my neck so I blew ever so softly into it and immediately lost sight of the moving antlers. Deer are sneaky critters when they want to be. They will sometimes drop to their knees to move under obstacles, and I figured that buck had lowered its head, turned around and cautiously slipped away. Maybe I had blown too hard … or too soft … on the call. I couldn't figure it out, but after waiting about 10 minutes without seeing any movement, I placed the call back inside my jacket.

That very moment a giant 8-pointer stormed out of the sendero and circled downwind of my position. Nervously, I prayed the activated carbon in the Scent-Lok suit was gobbling up my human odor as it had done so many times before.

Then, a doe unexpectedly stepped into the picture opposite the buck. He froze, stretched out his neck, put his nose in the air and, with his ears laid straight back, made directly for her. The chase ended within seconds as the big buck passed within 19 yards of my stand and committed suicide on my arrow.

Deer management is less difficult inside an 8-foot fence, but the concept is the same. Reduce the does, increase the quality of feed available to the herd, supplement the naturally occurring minerals and watch your bucks grow. The future of deer hunting lies in quality management programs such as the one at the Diamond K, and I was thrilled to take that buck.

In a normal year, deer may never need to drink free-standing water, taking sufficient water from abundant forbs and browse in their primary feeding areas.

With the introduction of a deer herd management plan that has a goal to produce big bucks, virtually any area of the US can build a healthy deer herd. To make such a plan work though, hunters have to stop harvesting little bucks and increase their take of does. Research by nationally recognized deer biologists Larry Marchinton and Karl Miller at the University of Georgia attest to the positive results of a management plan within only a few years.

Chapter 5

Getting Down To Business

Making a personal commitment to take only mature deer and big game is a life-altering experience. By now, you will have shared it with the necessary people, your family and hunting buddies, so before we go any further, I suggest you hang the certificate or contract on the wall of your workshop or glue it to the inside lid of your tackle box. Beyond your immediate circle of friends, it isn't going to be advisable or helpful to talk about your commitment, but you will often need to see the evidence of it to stay on track.

The real heroes of our sport are the ones who teach their youngsters the value of an outdoor lifestyle. Tim's daughters, Rachel (right) and Tara, understand his love of deer hunting, but they know that when he is in hot pursuit of deer, there is no tagging along for the fun.

Hunting is a passion and also a way of life. It is unlike a hobby such as stamp collecting or bonsai growing or woodworking, although people can certainly be passionate about their hobbies. Part of hunting is killing animals and in today's society, that sets us apart from the overwhelming majority of our fellow citizens.

Even though your intention to take only mature deer seems clear and honest and straightforward to you, some people, especially those who are not hunters, are not going to understand. These people are going to confuse the issue with ego, yours and theirs. They are going to listen and then think of you as a Trophy Hunter, someone who kills animals primarily to collect their antlers or hides, or perhaps as some Hollywood creation that kills for pleasure or just to get your name in a "record book." They are not going to understand the essence of the personal challenge and growth involved in your commitment unless they have been there themselves, and because we hunters are a small minority of the population these days, the chances of that are slim.

Arguing with people who are not hunters is almost always an unwinnable and frustrating endeavor. You can't liken your commitment to a quarterback who vows to take his team to the Super Bowl or a NASCAR driver who swears he's never going to lose the Daytona 500 again. In fact, your decision has very little to do with competition or with winning and losing in the conventional sense.

Your commitment may actually be more like someone trying to quit smoking: it is extremely difficult though not impossible. It is challenging and totally inside your own head. If you are in competition, it is competition with yourself, some part of you that is content to take the easy way. Even though that "done is good enough" part is very human and is actually inside all of us, it is hard to explain why you need to move beyond it, especially to strangers.

Now, likening your hunting commitment to stopping smoking may seem to put a negative spin on the mature-deer-only concept because you are not really trying to quit doing something, unless it is to quit taking small and immature deer home for dinner. Indeed, you are focusing your effort on doing something positive: growing yourself as measured by taking big deer.

So, my suggestion is to hold your commitment passionately but to put the certificate and your passion to make a change away from public view. Frame the paper where you can see it occasionally, but refrain from discussing it with anyone other than your spouse and close associates, including the people from whom you are going to begin asking for help and seeking information.

Finding The Right Spot To Hunt

There is a formula for successfully taking mature whitetails, and it takes a lot of factors into account, including your own efforts and the support of other folks. Successful bowhunters use quality equipment, excel in marksmanship and learn everything they can about whitetail behavior. They also learn and practice hunting techniques such as rattling and making a mock scrape, because it is a truism that we are part-time hunters while deer are wild and free.

Other factors in the success equation are continuous scouting, continuously watching for deer whenever you have a chance and finding productive places to hunt. Because we want to hunt better, not necessarily harder or longer, we are attentive to deer distribution in our neighborhood (i.e. we scout on a year-round basis). We hunt in part because we love the experience, but we do have to recognize our children and remember the anniversary. (You got married during hunting season! What were you thinking?) We hunt, perhaps to excess, but we do have a life that we must honor outside our hunting life.

The deer hunting solution is not half preparation, which includes year-round scouting, and half execution. It isn't even close. You are going to

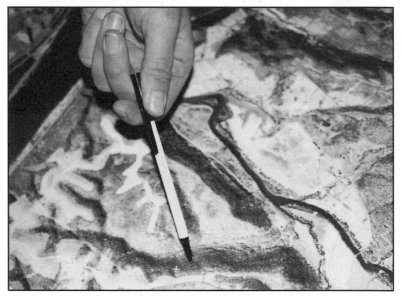

There are many indicators of the right spot to hunt: scrapes, rubs and even deer hair caught in a fence. All of these indicators plus your photos, sketches and interviews with local experts need to be compared to aerial photos of prospective sites.

spend a lot more time and effort and money to be prepared than you will in actual time on stand. Once you are prepared though, you still have to get outside and hunt; and for a mature animal, you have to either get very lucky or expect to do the hard work, just like you will have done already on the practice range and at your workbench. You could say that after all of the hours of preparation, it is finally time to take the fight to your opponent.

A wise old deer hunter once told me, "A hunter is only as good as the ground he hunts and the amount of time he puts in on stand."

I believe there is a lot of truth, some mystery and one false lead in that old-timer's statement. Hunters who consistently harvest trophy whitetails typically spend a lot of time in their stand. They hunt at every opportunity, but they keep in mind that the point is not time on stand. The point is effective time on stand, that intersection of time when a mature deer steps into your shooting lane. I believe that the single most important factor, number one in the trophy-deer formula, is not how much or how long one hunts, but the quality of ground.

Mature deer are everywhere. Grown-up deer, that is. Trophy deer, wall hangers, bucks with humongous racks. That's a different story. Let's recognize the truth. You have mature deer in your hunting area. The trick is to put oneself within shooting range of one of them on an annual basis. You may or may not have bucks with huge racks living in your neighborhood, though. To find big-racked deer takes a different type of focus. In this chapter, we're going to study the neighborhood first and the wider scheme of trophy whitetail distribution second. The objective is to find THE spot that will give you the best chance of harvesting a mature animal.

A Beautiful Day In The Neighborhood

After making your commitment, the first step is to begin the process of finding the right place to hunt. You have already been hunting someplace, just not the right place (or perhaps not the right way), and to accomplish your goal, to be the very best you can be, there is only the right place, the best place. Everywhere else is a waste of time and effort.

To begin, you are going to need information, and the best way to learn is to learn from other people, especially the local people who service and regulate the hunting community.

Now, there is a right way and a wrong way to enlist people in supporting your quest. Your inner circle of family and friends is best approached directly as they will take the time to listen and understand what you are talking about.

You need to approach people outside your inner circle of confidants indirectly, however. Remember that the best way for you to achieve a goal is to be interested in and to help other people realize their goals, even though few people will ever have set out their goals so succinctly and explicitly in writing as you.

Rule number one should be NOT to say something like, "Hi, I'm looking for the best place to take a trophy deer." The response is going to be, "Well, aren't we all."

People will be inclined to help you if you ask for their help with subjects that are within their areas of expertise. Your challenge is to think in advance of how you want to allow people to help you. With a taxidermist, for instance, you want to get his opinion on how to handle a deer so you can bring in a cape and rack in the best condition possible even if you think you already know the answer. Can he show you some examples of good handling and improper handling? Getting people to help you, people who may or may not have anything to gain by your success, puts you squarely on the sleuthing trail and the delicate path of diplomacy.

Whatever your choice of weapon, good preparation includes the use of a reliable range-finder, which eliminates the guesswork and allows you to focus on the task at hand.

Become A Deer Detective

Remember that you have made a commitment to take mature deer rather than the first thing that comes along. You want a healthy set of antlers or at least the dominant doe. Whether it makes the record books or not is beside the point, at least for the time being. Your job is to work your way up – or perhaps down – the food chain.

You have a lot to do. You must put together gear that's going to make your job easier and then become proficient with it. You have to begin a conscientious reading and learning program about whitetails and especially those in your area. It is a big job, but you volunteered, you made a commitment, you put it in writing and you shared it with your friends and family. Nobody else made you do this. Now get with it.

So, you have a lot to do, and you can do some of it simultaneously while you are finding the right place to hunt. This means you need to scout out your neighborhood thoroughly and expand your search if you don't find precisely what you are looking for. After that, you need to be prepared to continue expanding. Your buddies, remember, will be perfectly happy with the old familiar spots, but you cannot be happy with them and move your hunting to the next level. Move on.

Indeed, it is a beautiful day in the neighborhood!

How long should you expect to work at finding the right place to hunt? As long as it takes.

How far should you expect to have to travel? As far as you need to go to get the job done.

Caveat #1

Mature deer live everywhere there are deer, but some areas struggle to keep them alive long enough for them to reproduce more than once or grow their antlers to the full size possible given their genetic potential and the area's nutritional availability. If your county is heavily hunted, the chances that it will hold many big, mature deer are reduced, because pressure from hunters with guns and bows, muzzleloaders and crossbows, and road traffic during the rut will keep mature deer numbers low.

Hunting pressure is a huge issue. The amount of pressure an area experiences can be a significant problem for the deer herd where hunters resist shooting does, where traditionally they would rather take button bucks and spikes than a healthy female. When the buck-to-doe ratio deteriorates, even the most skilled hunter is going to have to work to take a big mature animal. But that's okay. You are probably working hard now without having too much to show for it.

How do you know whether there are sufficient numbers of mature animals in your area to merit the time you need to spend finding them? You know because you observe and you ask. You hang out with hunters and listen to their stories. You see what they kill, most hunters not being shy to show off their harvest. On the other hand, you have to make a decision where to draw the line. Here's what I mean.

Hunters who consistently take big deer will be reluctant to tell you where they are hunting. You could spy on them, but it would be beneath your dignity to follow them, uninvited, into the woods or somehow invade their favorite hunting territory.

Russell Hull of Hill City, Kansas, who published *Trophy Bowhunting: The Supreme Challenge* in 1984, told me that other hunters would wait down the street in his neighborhood and follow him to his best hunting spots, which were, by the way, on public land. If he stopped for gas, they stopped for gas. If he tried to throw them off his trail, he would get to the woods late, and the men following him would wait for him the next morning at 3 a.m. These individuals were not the least bit shy.

I'm no stranger to this phenomenon. I have been followed to hunting spots on numerous occasions. So, because everyone knows my truck, my wife has now become – among many other invaluable and inestimable roles in my life – my favorite chauffeur. I tease her about becoming a member of a US Navy SEAL team. Her job is to push me out of the truck, make the insertion, deliver the goods, and then, when the mission is complete, she swoops in to make the extraction, pick me up. Usually she arrives under the cover of darkness and totally covertly!

While I don't recommend that you pursue your mature deer objective in a shy manner, I absolutely do not recommend that you become an outlaw or a nuisance to other hunters in pursuit of your trophy goals. If you don't take your personal commitment seriously and make it work with integrity, you won't value it when you have achieved it.

Now, if Russell ever gives a hunting seminar or offers to give a tour of his trophy sites, sign me up. Otherwise, I wish him and all the other hunters who have already achieved their goals the very best. Now, it is our turn. Remember that if it were easy, everyone would be killing big, trophy deer and then maybe it wouldn't be fun any more.

On the other hand, there are many under-hunted lands in the public domain. Spots on wetlands management areas, for instance, do not "belong" to one individual unless he or she is there first the morning you stumble through their shooting lanes. You have as much right to scout and hunt as anyone else, so if you believe that someone is quietly taking big deer out of a public area near you, get in there and see what you can find out. Just do it legally and ethically.

You should consider conversations with area wildlife professionals, taxidermists and even other hunters as part of your scouting routine.

Enlist The Specialists

You know about your neighborhood because you make it a point to get to know your area's game warden, taxidermists, sporting goods store managers and archery pro shop owners. Individuals who routinely deal with hunters are wells of information and you can't afford to overlook them.

There is specific information you want from these professionals. Primarily, you want to know the location of the very best place to hunt for mature deer in your area. But that's not all you want. These specialists work full time in a field that you have decided to come to grips with. There is so much they can help you with – about loading for speed and accuracy, or bow tuning, or that secret spot that is not marked on the official state map – that will make your hill climb easier.

Although I have found that law enforcement types – and this definitely includes wildlife enforcement people – are by and large a difficult group to get to know or pry information from, they are outside in the woods almost every day and many nights. Very few people will have a better understanding of the wildlife resources in your neighborhood than a warden.

A game warden is a fine person who has a difficult job. Your job is to find a way to relate to someone who is predisposed to be suspicious of every hunter and fisherman. After a few years in the field, his tendency is to believe that everyone who has a license is a violator and his job is to simply discover the violation. I believe that many wardens are pressured to write

Even the most observant hunter will benefit from another set of eyes and the assistance of another hunter who understands your commitment.

citations for a greedy government bureaucracy because this is the income part of their work. Such an approach to wildlife management and enforcement usually does not make for a jolly, talkative buddy.

So, as you would with a difficult boss, your job is to find a way to relate without appearing to "suck up" to area wildlife people. Are they members of your church? Do they have kids in your school district? Where do they live and is there something of particular note or interest about their neighborhood that you can talk about? Has an article or photograph recently appeared in a newspaper about a trophy deer or huge fish from their area of responsibility? If so, were they quoted? What can they tell you about it?

Their job is to know their territory intimately; your job is to pry useful information out of them. Nevertheless, an open, friendly and up-front approach is always the first, best way to get on someone's wavelength. Asking for their help may work, but in my experience, these professionals hold their cards close.

Perhaps your first stop should be to get to know the taxidermists in your area. Who better knows what big deer have been taken in the neighborhood than the guys who build the mounts for the wall?

Taxidermists, like accountants or school teachers, come in all shapes, sizes and abilities. If he (or she) is good, he deals with the very best and very worst of the world of hunting. He turns the remains of a kill, stuff we

Watch bulletin boards in area taxidermy studios, pro shops and sporting goods stores for photos of successful hunters and then talk to them. Respect their privacy, but now is not the time to be shy!

can't eat, into a work of art. Meanwhile, he has time to socialize with his hunting and fishing clients. Shouldn't you try to tap into that knowledge? Besides, you will soon be taking a rack and cape to one of them and the better you get to know them, the better you know what to expect, what to insist upon and what quality you can afford.

There are limits, but be sure not to choose your taxidermist on the basis of price alone. Almost any location in the US will have several within driving distance and some areas will have dozens! Before I got truly serious about hunting, I had a couple mounts done by the cheapest taxidermist I could find, and now, a dozen or so years later, these bad boys are in the garage waiting for the rainy day when I take the antlers to be re-mounted.

Your next stop is to locate and get to know the shooting and hunting retailers in your area, not just the closest one. These people and their department managers and counter staff will know their steady and successful customers. If you are sincere about seeking their advice and asking for information, chances are they will come through with a lot of valuable tips. Many stores have maps and bulletin boards with pictures of customers holding their bucks. Get on their mailing list. Find out about the seminars they host. Then ask about those pictures on the wall.

This suggestion does not include the hourly workers at the *BoxMarts*. Fine people I'm sure, but when it comes to giving serious hunting (or fishing) advice, my experience is that they can't find the seat of their pants with two hands and a mirror.

Do you need to be a paying customer to win the trust and loyalty of a small business owner? Not necessarily, but it sure doesn't hurt. If you are serious about taking mature, trophy deer, you immediately want to give up shopping at the *BoxMart* and buying at discount prices over the Internet and through the heavily advertised mail-order stores. Your local sporting goods retailer may not have on hand everything that you want, but he can and will order it for you. Be a little patient. Patronize your local pro shops. Yes, you will pay more for a particular item. A Bodoodle arrow rest that costs $29.95 from some discount Internet site (plus $7.00 shipping and handling and a week to 10 days of waiting) may cost $42.00 plus sales tax at a pro shop, for instance. But what good is that extra six dollars going to do in your pocket if it could buy you a commercial acquaintance that is willing to help you? The few extra dollars will be a small price to pay for shooting and hunting tips.

And yes, it will be necessary to get up out of your easy chair, place your latest issue of *Deer & Deer Hunting* on the coffee table and drive to these stores. As I have said, what you are going to gain is far more valuable than the extra few dollars you are going to spend, and the time and effort are

The results of many of your dedicated efforts will be racks on the wall. Eventually, you will learn to let marginal bucks grow up.

part of your challenge, because the act of taking mature deer every year is not an antiseptic act. You have chosen to immerse yourself in a personal quest or challenge that, as corny as it sounds, entitles you to be a part of an elite brotherhood.

Should you limit yourself to the closest sporting goods store? Of course not! In a metropolitan area, there may be a dozen or more stores to visit. Learn the names of the people who set up and tune the bows, who repair firearms. Make a "cheat sheet" if you have to. Then spend time in their stores weighing the pros and cons of their inventory; and occasionally, drop a dime to shoot on their lanes.

It has always been my opinion that the best way to learn and improve my hunting and shooting was to practice and learn from others. The guys behind the counters fixing the bows, matching arrows to draw weights and tuning rests are the guys who do the hands-on work with hunting gear every single day. Unless they're total knuckleheads, they are the experts, and in the course of their work, they shoot the breeze with lots of people.

You also know whether your area holds big deer because you do the extra work of looking through newspapers, magazines and state publications for photos and reports. If you live in a city of any size, your newspaper will only want to report on the jock sports: basketball, football, baseball and hockey. It's easier for the newspaper to download wire service reports and do a little re-writing than to actually go out and dig up an interesting story. Besides, re-writing what is essentially free material fills space cheaply and publishers like cheap. Plus, the multi-million dollar athletic jocks have become celebrities. They have tattoos and attitudes. Their photos are published in the grocery store tabloids. Barbara Walters interviews them, and sometimes they literally get away with murder. (The age demographic of young men in their 20s and 30s, the big spenders for new personal watercraft and vanity sports items, unfortunately, supports the publisher's choice. Go figure. We're not successfully recruiting these "kids" into the shooting sports.)

If your area newspaper prints any honest-to-goodness outdoor coverage, it will certainly be infrequent, on the back page and primarily inoffensive fishing stuff. Well, the back page is better than nothing. It will be the unusual daily newspaper that runs any real hunting features. Like their jock cousins, many (but not all) outdoor writers for newspapers specialize in re-writing product press releases from manufacturers because it is … what? Cheap and easy. Right. Plus, these days if they ran a photo of a hunter with a beautiful buck he had just killed, the paper would get a hundred letters from tennis-shoers, little old ladies, woods fairies and animal rights activists. They just won't risk offending these people.

A polite letter to the sports editor asking that the paper increase its coverage of hunting and fishing is always a good thing, but don't expect any results or even a polite response without massive grass-roots pressure. It helps if sporting goods stores in the area insist on coverage. If they do insist, the threat to advertising revenues is obvious, and this goes directly to the heart of the 21st-century newspaper (and magazine!) business philosophy. Cheap and easy.

The very best sources of written information about your area may be small newspapers such as hometown weeklies and the locally produced,

Because Tim keeps a log of his hunting and scouting activities, he has a firm basis for evaluating the possibilities of alternate hunting locations if the weather changes or if timber-harvesting suddenly begins near his favorite woods lot.

newsprint-quality magazines you find in front of convenience store check-out counters. Every state has a number of specialized publications that deal with hunting and fishing. Sometimes you can find them at pro shops, but the magazine racks at gas-and-grocery stores usually have several that specialize in your state. They may be printed on lower-grade paper, often only in black and white, but they will have more information you can use in one issue than the daily paper will carry all year. These special publications will publish dozens of dark, grainy and out-of-focus pictures of people with their trophy deer and wowser fish. Plus, they will have names and will often give general locations where a hunter took a deer. You've all seen these: "Joe Smith of Smallville took this nice 10-point buck in Taylor County while he was hunting with his father, Bill, who owns the hardware store there." It's local and it may be folksy, but it is almost always 100 percent dead-on.

Your local outdoor publications will have telephone numbers listed inside on about page four in what is called the "masthead." This is where the editor, the advertising manager and their writers or correspondents are listed. Call them. Introduce yourself. If they will make a few minutes available, make an appointment and go see them. Don't be shy. Ask for their recommendations and advice. Then ask them to autograph an editorial or a story for you. If you are sincere, they will be flattered.

An additional and often overlooked source of information is your state game and fish department's Internet site (see Appendix #1). These sites vary tremendously in the quantity and quality of information available on them, but many contain wonderful insights into your state's deer environment. A PDF document on the Ohio site at www.dnr.state.oh.us/wildlife for example not only publishes the rules and regulations for hunting, but also lists Ohio wildlife officers by county. Inside that same document is a county map of Ohio showing deer harvest statistics for 2002-03 AND, important to your mission, the 1958-2002 statistics for trophy bucks registered by the Buckeye Big Buck Club, again by county!

When your dad took you hunting, you had to go downtown to the hardware store to buy your license. You can still do that, although the local hardware store is barely hanging on because of competition from *BoxMarts*. Today, the Internet provides an easier and virtually painless way to apply, and if you are shopping around for a great, out-of-state hunting spot, the Internet should be the first place you turn.

One of the radio stations in your area, probably an AM station, will give fish and game reports or perhaps read a fish and game forecast that is correlated with moon phase and tides. These stations are good for the occasional interview with an area game-control officer or even a hunter or fisherman. If you find such a radio goldmine, and they are more common in rural than in urban areas because they will also give reports on crop and cattle futures, it is very important for you to let them know you listen.

If you are in doubt about where to tune your radio and get tired of the crackle of static, check with a local feed and seed store (not the one for bird watchers, the one for farmers). Ask them where they advertise on the radio and then tune in. You can expect country music and conservative talk-radio hosts. If a steady diet of classical or opera is your preferred music fare when you are inside your vehicle, you are out of luck in this category.

Write It Down

I'm a big believer in writing things down. I find that it helps if I keep a notebook, and I believe this practice will help you, too. I can always go to that notebook for names and telephone numbers or addresses, for instance.

My advice is to get into the habit of systematically writing down (at least in note form) your observations and conversations, names and telephone numbers. Then you won't be jumping to conclusions every time you come across a lead. You won't be forgetting, "Oh jeez. What was that guy's name?"

Writing things down also helps you approach your challenge methodically – not boring, methodical. They are not the same. Methodical and systematic are the surest, straightest, fastest way to your goal, but if you are the standard, Grade-A-impatient, testosterone-driven male, this is not going to be easy. After all, you never had to ask for directions, and you have fought this since you picked up your first pencil in Miss What's-Her-Name's kindergarten class. So, it's certainly optional, but it's a darn good idea, and in the long run, it will make a big difference in the time and aggravation spent in achieving your hunting goals.

Caveat #2

I have already mentioned that one of the reasons your neighborhood might not hold trophy deer is because of heavy hunting pressure and a generations-old reluctance to shoot does. That reluctance, incidentally, stems from the early part of the 20th century when deer herds in many areas were on the brink of elimination. Rest assured that deer herds are by and large healthy today and the hunting harvest is sustainable in spite of occasional problems like the current eruption of chronic wasting disease.

There are several other reasons your area may hold very few big, mature deer. Some areas in the West don't have whitetails at all, even though this brilliant and adaptable species is expanding rapidly into mule deer habitat across the high plains and into the river bottoms throughout the West. Some areas in the South have a sub-species of whitetail that is just naturally small in body size and in its delicate antler configuration. If you live in south Florida, your definition of a mature deer may be any full-grown buck that has avoided being run over on the highway rather than a 250-pounder with a thick 12-point rack. There just aren't any of those humongous deer in that area, maybe not in the whole state!

Some areas are hit hard with chronic wasting disease (CWD) and other wildlife disease problems. This condition may be temporary or it may not be, but you are ready right now, not 5 years from now when CWD subsides or when we and Mother Nature find a solution.

If hunting becomes extremely difficult in your area because of one of these factors, do not waste your time there. Begin work immediately to find another place to spend your valuable time because, let's face it, if a 365-day year has 8760 hours and you spend 6 weekends (2 days each for a total of 12 complete days) a year in the field hunting from sunup to sunset (12 hours a day), you will only have spent 144 hours trying to fulfill your commitment. That's only 1.64 percent of your year! That's not much

Whether you are searching for mature whitetails, mule deer or pronghorn antelope, if you can spend time scouting from a distance, it will keep your primary hunting area undisturbed.

and probably is not enough, either. Hence, it is an absolute necessity to immediately abandon places that your research suggests are not going to be productive.

The bottom line is that no matter how knowledgeable or skilled you become, if you are hunting an area that doesn't hold mature bucks and does, the result will be nil. With this in mind, this chapter may quite possibly be the most important chapter in this book as well as the most beneficial to the reader who has become frustrated in their hunting spots or with their crowd of hunting buddies.

Create Your Own "Honey Hole"

I would be remiss if I didn't mention the possibility of acquiring your own little slice of heaven. Yes, actual SOIL of your own that you can tinker with; true outdoor HABITAT that you can "improve and manage for mature deer."

I'm referring to joining or forming a "hunting club" with folks you hunt with season after season. The hunt club models that work best are programs like Quality Deer Management (QDM) and Deer Management Application Program or DMAP. I have participated in each as a manager and a hunter and in both cases with outstanding results. Each has specific guidelines that must be followed for optimum results: total acreage, how to identify and treat bedding areas, development of food plots and supplemental planting/feeding, mineral supplements, escape cover/sanctuary, aging deer, harvest requirements and so on.

Getting involved in a deer management program has been one of the most rewarding aspects of my commitment to take only mature deer. Seeing the results of years of hard work is eminently satisfying and makes all the work worthwhile.

In 1998, my very good friend Lou Haubner and I began a deer management program on Lou's farm in southwest Ohio. Prior to that year, the bucks taken were mostly 1-1/2 years old. They averaged six to eight points. After implementing a management program for four seasons, the average buck killed was 2-1/2 years and sported eight to 10 points. As of this writing, the average mature buck sighted is a 3 1/2-year old that will probably score 135 to 140 P&Y/B&C. There are even a few in that special 4-to-5-year category scoring 150 and above! A great book with much more information about deer management programs is *Quality Whitetails* by Karl Miller and Larry Marchinton. You can also check out Internet sites such as *www.qdma.com.*

Chapter 6

The Five Secrets Of Effective Scouting
Part 1

There are only five secrets to finding mature deer. I have distilled these five essential ideas from a lifetime of experience. The last half of that life – or about 25 years – has been eyes-wide-open hunting because I long ago made a commitment to take only mature deer. I am not interested in little deer, in button bucks and immature animals, except to wish them well and as general indicator that deer are present, but I will take a big doe every now and then when the freezer needs re-stocking.

Number 1 – Expand Your Horizons

If you wanted to learn a language like Italian, what would the best way to do that? Obviously, you should travel to Italy and live there. Have nothing to do with English until you are perfectly fluent. It would take maybe a year or two until you could converse easily with the Italians about subjects from sex to rocket science.

The next best way to learn Italian is to take formal in-school classes where you are subjected to the rigors of an instructor's discipline. But we are grown men and women with jobs and children and homes to take care of and unscheduled time is scarce. Realistically, the best that most of us will be able to do is an un-graded community college class or maybe an informal study group.

The third way is not the best or easiest way to learn Italian, but it is practical and it will eventually work if you stick with it. If you make a commitment to learn a few words or one element of grammar or sentence structure every day, by the end of a year or when you are ready to travel to Italy, you should be able to converse and read enough to get by in restaurants and hotels and at most tourist destinations. If you keep this routine up for two, or three, or five years, you will eventually become fluent.

When he gets the chance, Tim always takes time to learn from other knowledgeable hunters, like Terry Rohm.

Learning to harvest mature whitetail bucks is like learning a foreign language after you are an adult. You cannot live in the woods with the deer herd. Only the extraordinary individual could survive for an extended time alone in the wilderness. You can, however, take occasional informal classes by attending deer expos, going to seminars and continuing the reading you are doing now. Just do not call your local school board or library and ask for a class schedule for deer hunting. Seminars are wonderful for fresh ideas, for mentally pumping you up ("If that fool with the microphone can do it … ") and for getting your internal engine revved. Nevertheless, relearning your hunting strategy is a day-to-day process, much like learning a foreign language one word or phrase at a time. Sorry. For most of us, there is no shortcut.

You may read that it helps to scout in the camo you wear during the season and that you should take practice shots from your stand to judge distance and get warmed up. Bad advice, Tim says. Save your camo for hunting, and when it becomes worn or faded, destroy it. Never go to your prime hunting area for shooting practice and use a rangefinder.

So, any time you read that scouting for deer is a year-round activity you can bet that the writer understands what he or she is talking about … almost. In my experience though, hunters become stuck in a very deep rut: they hunt and they scout the same place year after year. This is exactly what I did for many years. Time after time, I have shot little deer and then gone right back to that spot the next year and done it again, not even moving my stand to a different tree. I would make one or two trips to the woods during the pre-season when the foliage was thickest (and when the bugs were thickest, too) and have a general look around to see if anything major had changed and I would call it scouting. I had a clue, but not a plan.

Of course, in my early years, I was thrilled to take a button buck with a bow. My father was a gun hunter and a good one, but in our family the bow was uniquely mine. So, a button buck was a trophy to me. Then I realized that more experienced hunters were just being kind to the kid when they admired my little deer and told me what a fine hunter I was. Well, that phase did not last, and I learned that to be the quality of hunter I want to be I had to be open to new possibilities. I had to have a year-

Scout with a purpose. If you simply go into the field because you "have not been out there in a while," you are wasting your time and may permanently spook the deer. Do not waste your time. Have a specific objective every time you go to your prime hunting area.

round learning and hunting program, maybe a life-long program even though that makes it sound like I'm in school forever (and that is not a pleasant thought).

If I said that you needed to spend some time scouting for deer every week and every month though, I would only be partly right, but I would be partly wrong. You do not need to get out into the woods for a day every month, because that is a guilt trip waiting to happen. You just need to do your scouting in the woods at the right time of year. I think our problem is the definition of "scouting" that we have become accustomed to reading about.

People who think that scouting for deer means they have to get out in the woods and walk around every month have too limited a definition or idea of what effective scouting is all about. Walking around in the woods you hunt and "looking at stuff" is fine, but before you go, you ought to decide what it is that you want to see and learn. Otherwise, unless you also think of it as good exercise in the outdoors, you are simply wasting your time and disturbing the area.

In a former chapter, I said you needed to spend some time getting to know your area and the people in it so that you can make informed decisions. This is the basic principle of true scouting. You want to get to know the wildlife officers (the game wardens) if possible and the taxidermists and the folks behind the counters at sporting goods stores. Information that these people give you is going to help you narrow your focus of areas to hunt for mature deer.

Within a reasonable driving distance of where I live, there are thousands of places I could scout. I would soon enough find deer in most of them, but I do not want just deer. I want big, mature deer. The people I mentioned above are some of the folks who can help you select and eliminate hunting spots.

And sure, if there is a guy in your area who regularly takes trophy deer, see if you can get to know him. Maybe he will let you buy him lunch. Ask him for hunting and shooting tips. Ask him to tell you the story of how he took the buck he was pictured with in the newspaper. You could even ask him where he hunts, but do not expect that he is actually going to tell you anything of substance. Who needs that kind of company when you are bowhunting?

Consider all of this non-woods interviewing and reading as scouting, just like pulling on your boots and tromping through the woods in February or March in an attempt to beat the squirrels and porcupines to shed antlers. Getting to know the right people in your area is going to be a lot more effective in terms of finding mature deer than wandering aimlessly around outside.

Number 2 – Have A Specific Plan

Unless you just enjoy a walk in the woods, why would you go out on a boots-on-the-ground scouting mission without an objective, without accomplishing part of your written plan? Take your notebook and a camera. If you do not have a plan, how are you going to know what you are looking for? Without a plan, you are just wandering around, like a tourist. Wear your Bermuda shorts and a Hawaiian shirt.

Now that I have said that, you do not want to become bogged down. Do not concentrate on making and writing down a plan to the point that you cannot move. Simply write down a few specific things you are looking for and as we go through this and the next couple of chapters, I will give you a few suggestions. Of course, there is a catch. The catch is that when you find what you are looking for, I am going to tell you to write that down in your notebook too. Not *War and Peace*, but at least a sketch map and a few notes you will be able to decipher later in the fall when the leaves change or there is snow on the ground. Things look different then. Things ARE different then.

If you understand what deer are eating and how the seasonal rotation of foods in the area affects their movements, you are well on your way to harvesting excellent deer. This photo was taken during the first year of quality deer management at River Ridge in Ohio: (left to right) Lamar Parker, Jerry Brucker, Lou Haubner and Tim Hooey.

Number 3 – Understand What Deer Are Eating And Why

Deer live near where they can eat and under normal conditions they eat every day, the peak of the rut and the middle of the winter being possible exceptions. Food is the most important element of on-the-ground scouting. You want to map out food sources available in the areas you have selected for closer study because while these foods will be seasonal, they will determine patterns of deer movement.

Food sources can be crops in farm fields or oak acorns or browse and forbs. For instance, if you are studying the edges of a cornfield for well-used entry and exit routes, recognize that if deer are not disturbed they will move in and out of the field casually. You should draw a little map sketch of the edges of the field and the trails that lead into and out of this deer dining room.

You are not ready to pick out stand sites yet, but keep an eye out for good locations between trails, back from the field. As deer move closer to the field, they become increasingly wary, especially after they first sense hunting pressure. They are more relaxed in the deeper sanctuary of the woods. Because you want your quarry to be comfortable, place your stands back in the woods no closer to the field edge than 75 or 100 yards. This depends on the configuration of the land and your own travel routes toward and away from your stand. We will talk more about terrain in a later chapter.

Probably sometime in September or October, farmers in your area are going to pick the corn. Then what? From visiting with them, you know which ones will leave some corn standing and which ones will turn the dead stalks under right away. Their farming practices can most definitely affect your hunting success.

Even with high-quality crops in the field – corn, soybeans, and clover – studies show that deer prefer naturally occurring foods such as white oak acorns and greenbrier. So, once farmers harvest their crops, effectively removing this temptation, the deer are going to rely on field scraps and then practically 100 percent on Mother Nature's own food sources. What are these in your area? Chances are that these will be dispersed rather than highly concentrated and that deer will travel more, spending more time in the woods and along roadways searching for edibles.

A great deal of work has been done on wildlife food plots in the past 10 years. Foods from other countries such as New Zealand have been imported. In spite of many commercial claims for exotic plants and clovers, food plots should never be thought of as more than supplements to naturally occurring foods. Remember that except in rare cases, deer prefer native foods to planted crops and exotics.

Is a food plot possible in your area? Will it attract deer? Will it attract big deer? My experience is that big, mature deer will occasionally use food plots although they are smart enough not to get caught in them.

You cannot tell what deer are thinking any more than you can tell if the neighbor tithes at church or your children are smoking at school. You can only make inferences and then take action based on the behavior you observed. Is there a smoky smell on your kids' clothes? Does the deer go first to the oak tree at the edge of the cornfield or does it head directly into the standing corn? Do deer prefer food that is good for them or do they eat because something tastes good to them at the moment? We humans, the so-called thinking species, don't always eat what is good for us, so why should we expect deer to make food choices based on inherent nutritional value?

This lone apple tree on the edge of a hayfield stands near excellent cover and bedding areas. Depending on the wind, Tim says, you should definitely consider a nearby set-up and then get ready!

Nutritional requirements for deer vary by season, by sex, by age and by physiological condition. A fawn has different needs than an adult buck or doe and a lactating doe has a different need than a buck growing trophy antlers. Deer nutritional needs do not vary, however, from one region of the country to the next. To reach its potential for body growth, health and antler size or, in the case of a doe, a healthy fawn, a deer in Florida needs roughly the same nutritional intake per pound of live weight as a deer in Alberta.

Deer are vegetarians. They are not carnivores like a wolf or an omnivore like a human. We humans will eat anything, but deer are "vegans" and that's all the more reason to kill and eat them. They eat four types of natural foods and these are the four you will pay attention to when you are out scouting: browse (woody plants), forbs (flowering weeds), cacti (in the south and southwest) and grass. Deer seem to prefer forbs such as bundle flower, ground cherry and lazy daisy, and these are most nutritious. Grass, normally the least important dietary element for deer, is con-

Locating a hot set-up near a trail between seasonal food sources and active bedding areas should be one of your primary objectives when you are scouting.

sumed in spring and fall when other plants have peaked or are not fully developed. Some plants, spring hackberry in Texas, for instance, offer high quality browse year round and are a significant source of protein, digestible materials and phosphorous.

When you are actively scouting, study pasture edges for deer, but watch the pasture or field itself for domestic animals. Deer live compatibly on the open range with cattle, horses and bison, for instance, but the dietary preferences of these animals are similar to those of sheep and goats, which will quickly reduce the food available to wild deer.

To reach their full potential, deer need the same things as humans, but because they are ruminants, vegetarians with a four-chambered stomach, they meet their needs in different ways. They need water, protein, carbohydrates (starch, sugar and fiber), lipids (fats and oils), minerals and vitamins. A lot of deer researchers include energy in this list, but energy is a product of some the above (protein, carbohydrates, fats and oils), not a basic consumable.

Water makes up about three-quarters of a deer's body weight and researchers estimate they need 3 to 6 quarts a day. While deer have been known to live for a month or so without eating, they can't go a week without drinking. In fact, after 3 dry days, a deer is in serious trouble. Cut a deer's water, and it will almost immediately stop eating and begin to lose weight.

Deer take on water in three ways: from so-called "free" water (drinking from a stream), from the water in the plants they eat (called "pre-formed" water) and from the water produced in their own cells, "metabolic" water. Measures of water content in typical deer browse in the South has ranged from 45 to 65 percent with as much as 70 to 90 percent in forbs (flowering weeds) and 90 percent in prickly pear cactus, which is a high-energy food source.

How deer take on water has an impact on your hunting strategy. If the year is wet and lush and the plants they eat are well watered, deer may not have to drink from streams or ponds at all! If you are hunting in a drought year when lack of rain turns the weedy ditches along farm roads to a blowing, dusty hell, putting up a stand near a well-worn trail where deer cross a stream will be a productive idea.

Protein is a key to growth, repair of damaged body parts, antler growth and routine health. In other words, like us, deer need protein to just keep on keeping on. Studies show that if there is insufficient protein in a deer's diet, there will almost certainly be insufficient antler to interest a hunter of mature bucks. Apparently, the growth and health of the body takes precedence over antler development, so less protein means smaller antlers (even though the deer itself may be healthy) and more protein in their diet usually means larger antlers.

Dietary studies suggest an adult deer needs between 13 and 16 percent protein throughout the year for optimum health. Many supplemental feeds and seeds touted for food plots advertise that they contain more protein than that, sometimes twice as much. A deer taking more protein is like a human overdosing on Vitamin C in the morning. There is a limit to the amount of C our body can actually use, and we're not sure how much protein a deer's body and antlers can use, but all things being equal, more protein allows a buck to reach its full genetic potential.

It defies logic that deer eat less in the winter. You would intuitively guess that they would eat more of whatever was available to keep their bodies heated and supplied with fuel. In fact, almost the opposite happens. While deer do eat in the winter, they eat less, and consequently, they end up consuming less protein during the cold months than at any other time of the year. Of course, less high-quality food is available in the winter, but deer also put on a layer of fat during the summer and fall from which to draw energy during the winter. In a harsh winter, deer draw the fat reserves down faster than in a mild winter.

Antlers, by the way, are about half protein. Before what is called "mineralization" or the hardening of the antlers occurs in about August, there

University research conclusively demonstrates that deer prefer natural acorns and forbs to corn or clover.

is a velvety covering over antlers that is almost 100 percent protein. (There are in fact some human medicinal functions for this velvet before it dries and withers.)

At the Grazingland Animal Nutrition Laboratory (GANSLab) at Texas A&M University, Scott Showers developed a predictive health equation for the deer that he studied near Nacogdoches, Texas (1996). Three ranges of nutrition were established for crude protein, digestible organic matter and phosphorous. Although it is crucial to health and antler growth, the phosphorous content always registered less than 1 percent.

Fawns *(already weaned from their mothers)*
Crude Protein (CP): For average growth and future antler development, fawns on average needed somewhere between 12 and 16 percent protein. A slight increase to 14 to 22 percent, however, predicted good to excellent growth and development.
Digestible Organic Matter (DOM): This is a rough measure of the energy output from the food they ate, and 50 percent was considered minimal for maintenance.

Yearlings and Mature Males
Crude Protein: A maintenance diet can be established with as little as 6 to 10 percent, but for optimum antler development, 13 to 16 percent is much better.
Digestible Organic Matter: A range of 50 to 60 percent maintains good health and grows antlers, too.

Females
Crude Protein: Maintenance standards are as little as 6 to 10 percent, increasing to 11 to 15 percent during gestation and remaining in the 14 to 22 percent range while lactating (feeding their fawns).
Digestible Organic Matter: Fifty to 60 percent is required at all times.

Much more can be learned from the Showers report, a summary of which is published on-line at www.cnrit.tamu.edu.ganlab (as of January, 2004). An important aspect of the study is that for only $25 the laboratory will give you a printout specific to the deer in your neighborhood. The lab's investigative procedure begins when you collect a sample of deer droppings and send it with the completed form from the on-line site to College Station where the Texas A&M GANSLab is located.

At GANSLab, technicians dry and grind the fecal sample you send them and then subject it to a test they call NIRS, for "near infrared reflec-

Whitetail clover is my favorite food-plot blend. This handful of ripe clover from a second-year food plot is held by Lou Haubner of River Ridge Farms.

tance spectroscopy." The resulting report, which they promise to have back to you within a couple days, tells you a great deal about the quality of food that the deer you sampled was consuming 36 hours prior to defecating.

NIRS information from Texas A&M was developed to help produce big cattle, but it can obviously be used almost as well for deer. If you plant food plots, for instance, the nutrients required can be directly supplemented. If you are hesitating to choose a hunting site, an evaluation of deer consumables in the area through this report could help you make up your mind. If your poop selection is a random pick-up, there is a small chance that you could have poop from an animal that is sick. You will not know whether it is a buck or a doe either, but that will not matter. The odds are, in a random universe, the deer droppings you pick up will be representative of the area and vegetative phase or time of year. If the GANSLab report indicates the protein in your sample is light or the energy available from digestible organic matter is low, you may want to find another place to hunt or you may choose to supplement the deer diet.

Another reason to keep scouting if your report comes back bad is that although the quality of natural foods increases during the months of summer, by autumn it is beginning to decline. Chances are you are sending in a fecal sample from prime scouting time, summer and early autumn. Well, it won't get any better.

In tests at Auburn University, whitetails preferred naturally occurring foods to planted crops. This study indicated that you could find deer in the Japanese honeysuckle, blackberry, dewberry, greenbrier and forbs year round, but only occasionally raiding the soybeans, cowpeas, American jointvetch, Alyceclover and corn.

Interestingly, the tests at Auburn suggested that you could dramatically enhance the quality of food available to deer – and presumably to other species as well – by fertilizing the naturally occurring forbs (what we think of as weeds) along roadsides, in fallow or old fields and along fencerows. Auburn recommended liming, application of a fertilizer and then a pass with ammonium nitrate for complete impact. This may only be practical on any significant scale for commercial hunting operations or well-endowed hunting clubs, but the study suggested that such a practice could push the crude protein content of the plants well beyond double their natural state!

The good folks at Auburn also suggested that it would be worth a hunter's time to fertilize mast-producing and wild-fruit-bearing trees like white oaks, swamp chestnut oaks, water oaks and persimmon, crab apple and wild grape. Fertilizing under the "drip line" – away from the trunk but under the canopy – was recommended at the time when new leaves begin to appear.

This shooting house over a green field could be an excellent spot for riflemen, but mature bucks usually will not venture close enough for archers or shotguns during normal shooting hours.

When it comes to carbohydrates, deer do not read the labels on the food they eat. They still live in the pre-carb days when more was better for active individuals. They eat very little starchy foods (like potatoes and carrots, for instance) but a lot of fiber (cereal grains, small twigs and even tree bark). Figure that an adult deer needs more than 3000 Kilocalories per day, year round. According to the experts, during the rut, like during the core of winter when food sources become scarce, both bucks and does reduce their food intake dramatically. As a result, in the rut and the immediately following winter months, deer can lose between 15 and 30 percent of their body weight.

If they do not eat much in the rut, which is generally in November, and they do not eat much during the winter months, when do they eat? The bulk of the food a deer consumes during the year is during the late spring, summer and early fall. The critical times are early spring and early fall. Food sources and food quality decline after September and do not begin to regenerate until April or May.

High-quality foods for deer include acorns from white oaks and forbs or what we normally think of as weeds.

What about the corn in your feeder? Deer are ruminants, and like dairy cattle, they need a fibrous diet to process their food. They could not exist for long solely on a concentrated ration of high-quality human food. A deer consuming a large pile of corn could go into toxic acidosis and many studies suggest that supplemental deer feeds should be food plots or pelletized, mixed-grain, high-fiber rations.

Lipids are fats and oils. Fats if they are solid at room temperature or oils if they are not. The lipids in a deer's diet are important for energy storage because they have 2.5 times the energy per gram as do proteins or carbohydrates. So, the oil in an acorn is very important. Deer milk, by the way, is 7.7 percent fat, which is nearly double that of cow's milk.

While it is true that deer build layers of fat during the summer and fall to prepare for winter, they do not need fat specifically in their diet to do that. They convert the energy in carbohydrates to saturated adipose (stored) fat and use that during hard times.

A distant hunt at a lodge that is well known for producing big deer will be expensive, but fun. Tim believes that if you think of the $2500 you will spend on such a hunt in the same manner that you might think of spending on a trip to Atlantic City or Las Vegas, you will probably not be disappointed.

If you decide to make an occasional trip to hunt at a commercial operation, trust your guides, but make sure – in advance – that they understand the difference between the needs of a gun hunter and those of a bowhunter.

Not a great deal is known about the mineral and vitamin requirements of deer. The total mineral content of a mature deer's body is about 5 percent, but the major minerals needed for good health and antler development, milk production, blood clotting and muscle contraction are calcium and phosphorous. Hardened, mineralized antlers are about 22 percent calcium and 11 percent phosphorous. Bucks apparently store minerals in their skeletons and transfer them to the antlers when needed. In other words, bucks undergo a form of osteoporosis or the removal of minerals from their bones, similar to that which happens in mature women. The difference is that after their antlers harden, the minerals lost from the bones are replaced directly from the diet.

As I mentioned earlier, energy (measured as calories or kilocalories (Kcal), 1 Kcal = 1000 calories) is not a food source nutrient, but a derivative of protein, lipids and carbohydrates, and an adult deer needs more than 3000 Kcal per day. While deer need energy, a study from Mississippi State University reports that the amount they need and use depends upon their age, sex, the weather and time of year. Calories are required for basal metabolism (breathing, maintaining body temperature, movement), but actual energy requirements are about twice the amount needed just to maintain life. There are, of course, additional energy requirements for growth, reproduction, pregnancy, lactation and antler development. Curiously, just standing up increases the energy demands on the body by 9 percent over lying down. You can try this at home!

Chapter 7

The Five Secrets Of Effective Scouting
Part 2

This is our boots-on-the-ground scouting chapter. Formerly, we talked about how you set the stage for work in the field by talking to informed professionals in the area(s) you are thinking about hunting. This helps you identify the specific area(s) on which you want to concentrate. We then talked about how important it is to have a plan with specific objectives if you are going to effectively scout for mature deer. Finally, we talked about deer nutritional requirements, the background information you need to identify natural sources of food and, hence, deer travel routes and bedding areas.

In this chapter, we will talk about how to get up and out of the armchair to search for the right sign in the deer woods. You will see the standard things – scrapes, rub lines, signs of bedding, game trails and deer themselves – and synthesize them in a manner that gives you a neighborhood activity chart for the deer around you. Your mission is to look as effectively or meaningfully as possible because you are not looking for just any deer. You are only hunting for mature, trophy bucks.

Now, Let's Face Facts!

You can read an article on some phase of scouting for deer in practically every hunting magazine you pick up from January through December. Most of what is written is pretty commonplace information, even a little stale, although the writers try to jazz up their ideas with hip terminology, such as "power scouting" or "scouting for super bucks." Nevertheless, the information is not much different than what the same magazine published the year before and maybe the year before that. I believe that most of what you read in these articles is thin advice, based perhaps on a little bit of personal observation and experience, but meager on the wildlife basics to back up their casual claims. "Hunt ridgelines for big bucks," one article will boast, for instance. The very next article says to pay particular attention to the small creeks and thickets in valleys between the ridges for those same big bucks.

Sure, big bucks are where you find them. But maybe you never stopped to think about the fact that the majority of the top trophy whitetail bucks listed in state record books or in the national B&C or P&Y books are taken by average guys who just happen to bump into them. The really humongous deer killed in the US and Canada every year are shot by hunters who never knew the deer were there, who never drew up a written plan and who had never before taken a trophy deer. Here are a few examples:

Big deer are everywhere. Friend Lou Haubner took this fine buck in southern Ohio after two years of intensive management to produce a healthy, high-quality deer herd.

Example #1

Jerry Brant did not think of himself as a trophy hunter, but he took an enormous 38-point non-typical whitetail with his crossbow in Fulton County, Illinois, on November 15, 2001. According to the Buckmasters scoring system, this buck measured a whopping 297 3/8, and Boone & Crockett measurers who scored it at 291 1/8 recognize it as one of the three biggest whitetails ever taken by a hunter anywhere with bow, gun or crossbow.

Jerry shot the buck at 15 yards, but that morning he had hoped for a shot at a wild turkey. After all, it was only a week or so before Thanksgiving. According to Mike Handley, who wrote the story for the September 2003 issue of *Rack*, neither Jerry nor his friend Fred had any idea that a buck that size lived in the area. They chose the stand site not because of deer sign but because they thought it gave them the best chance to kill a turkey. When he pulled the trigger of the crossbow, Jerry had just finished eating a Hostess Twinkie and had an open can of Mountain Dew in his lap! He thought, "I just hope I don't spill my soft drink."

Example #2

In 2002, Brian Osowski invited his friend Peter Kiendzior to hunt at a buddy's camp in Massachusetts. It was cold and snowing. Using a topographic map, Peter decided that since everyone else was hunting low, in the swamps and heavy pines, he would hunt a high ridge covered with tangles of brush (he called them "slashings") and blowdowns. Within hours, he pulled the trigger of his shotgun on a new Massachusetts number one record whitetail. Peter said his "jaw dropped" when he realized how big the deer was.

The group of hunters carried the buck to a check station and then to B&G's Sporting to get owners Bill and Marie Gogal's help. Bill and Marie took pictures and gave them information on registering the huge buck – an eight by six with three drop tines in front and a horn curled backward "on top" – with the state of Massachusetts and the name of an official scorer for the Northeast Big Buck Club and the Boone & Crockett Club. According to the August 2003 *Whitetail Hunting Strategies*, Peter's non-typical buck green-scored 207 5/8 and would likely replace the 60-year old record of 202.

Example #3

Don Baldwin only had to walk 150 yards from his back door near Bay City, Michigan, to his treestand to arrow an enormous buck in 2002. He could have taken it in 2001, but Murphy – yes, the Murphy of Murphy's Law – was present that day and gave unwelcome assistance. So, on October

17, 2002, Don left his auto repair shop early to go hunting. He sprayed thoroughly with an odor neutralizer, picked up his archery gear and rattling antlers and set off.

Don reported that he did a lot of pre-season scouting and told Rick Asmus, writing for the September 2003 issue of *North American Whitetail*, that he thought he had figured out the big buck's movement from a bedding area to a woodlot filled with mature oak trees. On October 17th, Murphy put in an appearance again, but the buck stood around until Don finally arrowed him, at only 10 yards after he had gotten down from his stand for the evening! Don jumped up and down screaming when he found the deer later that evening and realized how big it was. The 7-1/2-year-old deer scored 192 2/8 net and field dressed at 207 pounds.

What this is all about is average guys taking big deer. The three examples I have cited above are from Illinois, Massachusetts and Michigan. They could just as easily have been from Mississippi, Oklahoma or Montana. They illustrate that big-name hunters are not the people who consistently take the great deer. In bowhunting, our beloved Fred Bear took trophy tigers and elephants and sheep from Alaska, but not whitetails. It is a little different in the gun world because of the relative ease of shooting accurately at great distance. For whitetails taken by fair-chase methods, average working guys like you and me are just as likely as anyone to take a terrific deer.

After you read a few dozen stories about the guys who set new standards for their state trophy books, you begin to recognize that about two-thirds of them never had a clue that a trophy deer was in the area. They were just out lollygagging in the woods (like you used to do) when a monster walked by and they shot it. Congratulations to them. Seriously. However, unless these people are particularly gifted in a special place to hunt or are rich, they will never shoot another great big deer the rest of their life.

What we are talking about and what I am laying out a strategy for is taking big, mature deer every year and doing it consciously. We're talking about learning. We are good at that. It is something very near and dear to our hearts as human beings – learning by trial and error, thinking our way through the steps, changing our methods if one approach does not work and gradually, consciously working our way closer and closer to our goal.

So, unless you live in Death Valley or in downtown Manhattan and never venture outside the suburbs, you have a chance of taking a mature deer every year. Even if you do nothing different at all, read not another word of this book, you still have a chance of taking a world-record whitetail. It happens, but chances are that unless you prepare consciously, Murphy will help you screw it up. That's why we are hunting strategically and that begins with strategic scouting.

Number 4 – Strategic Scouting: Putting Boots On The Ground With A Purpose

We began this chapter talking about all the articles written in magazines about scouting for deer and have so far tried to demonstrate that you can take a huge deer even if you pay no attention to the suggestions in this book, even if you never read another story about scouting for deer or even if you go hunting blindfolded. Except for the blindfold, it happens. But most likely, from a statistical point of view, that little miracle will never happen to you, or if it does, it will only happen once in your life.

The magazine stories I am talking about are the ones that encourage you to pull your boots on and get out on the ground you will be hunting as much as possible before the season. Most of them give advice that will not hurt your hunting too much, so my point is that they all say about the same thing:

Not just a deer hunter, Tim has an opportunity to travel throughout North America to bowhunt. "A distant hunt every now and then can really spice up your hunting year," Tim says.

1. Walk your hunting area and look for deer sign every chance you get.

2. Drive around to: a) Look for deer and b) so that you know what developments may change the pattern of deer movement: new houses, changes in crops, expansion of roads, etc.

3. Get aerial photos and topographic maps if you are hunting in a large or unknown area such as a large wildlife management area that is open for public hunting.

4. Study the record books for tips on where to hunt.

I want to spend a few minutes discussing these four items, letting you in on their secrets and what they really mean to your specific hunting possibilities and to your commitment to take only mature deer.

Except for exercise and the sheer joy of being outside, walking around aimlessly in your hunting area is pointless. If it does more than temporarily interrupt the area's natural rhythms and disturb the resident deer, it can be downright harmful. So, you must have a plan.

How could scouting for deer possibly be harmful? Several reasons. You are leaving your scent throughout the area, and while deer may not be as quick, generally speaking, to learn as humans, big deer are quick to learn when it comes to their home range. Much like we would be if strangers wearing strange cologne ambled through our dining and bedrooms every now and then. Learning is how big deer get to be big. As you go through the woods, you disturb the foliage, and if you are pre-selecting a couple of trees for stands because they look good – because they are straight and about the right diameter and about right in relation to a trail or the edge of a field – you might as well burp out loud at your mother-in-law's Thanksgiving dinner. And if your size 10 boots are tromping through the underbrush while you are only checking out the tweetie birds, you are inevitably going to look down and see the soft depressions made by deer sleeping and hiding during the day. Check 'em out. They may still be warm. You have run these deer out of their "bedrooms," and they will not soon return.

Driving around a hunting area and watching for deer to come out into a field is a very good idea ... or it used to be, in a more open and trusting society. These days, sad but true, you ought to be sure you have a photo ID, and if you are sitting along a roadside with binoculars or a spotting scope – unless you are in the middle of Manitoba or some desolate spot in Oklahoma – it is going to help to know thy neighbors. If you have a firearm or bow and arrow, they better be locked away in the trunk or inside a gearbox unless you are performing this scouting mission in the daytime during hunting season (and even then you need your license handy). Otherwise, expect a set of blue flashing lights to be paying you a visit and calling in

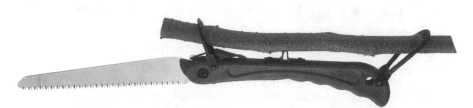

Tim always carries a pocket saw when he scouts in the "off season," but with his commitment for taking big deer every year, there is very little "off season." Trim carefully, he says, and make no cuts near the opening of the hunting season.

your tag number to HQ. Usually, in the country, you are going to be fine if you are properly licensed, but with America's heightened state of security consciousness since 9-11, it pays to be more obvious rather than less so.

There is nothing inherently wrong with this kind of four-wheel scouting and on a few occasions, I have seen a mature buck come out into a clear-cut or a farm field. A power-line right-of-way can provide a good vantage point also. This practice is pretty 1960s, and it isn't extremely productive unless you have plenty of hours to kill. Unless you are glassing during the rut (when almost anything can happen), you know that a mature deer is going to wait to appear in the open until it feels secure, and that means after dark. During the rut, a buck is liable to follow a doe through the drive-in at a McDonalds fast food joint, but if you have done your scouting properly, this is a moot point. You will know about where the bucks are at any given time of day and there won't be any reason to park along a road and glass open fields.

Of course, there is one specific reason to drive roads in your hunting area. That is to make a base map of food sources and travel routes and to revise your map for any changes since you began hunting there. Food sources might be standing corn or soybeans, someone else's wildlife food plots or stands of acorn-bearing oaks. Even if your hunting spot is a small block of woods in the middle of a sea of planted fields, you will be able to plot drainage ditches or brushy fence lines that can help you understand how and where deer move during the hunting season. Deer will use these ditches and fence lines and they are wonderful places to search out for a stand or even a ground blind.

I have talked about making and using a map, on a real piece of paper, and not just trying to keep a general idea of the area in your mind. Now, I recognize that a lot of us refuse to even ask for directions if we are lost, so when you hear "make a map," you go "yeah, sure, okay"; but this is a serious step if you want to begin taking mature white-tailed deer every year. I can't tell you how many times I have looked at my sketched-up maps and made changes or put in something that I hadn't thought of before and suddenly the light bulb came on and I went, "oh – now I see" and then went out and found the deer I was looking for. More than once! So make a map and use it. I guarantee that it will help you learn your area better ... and you do not have to tell anyone.

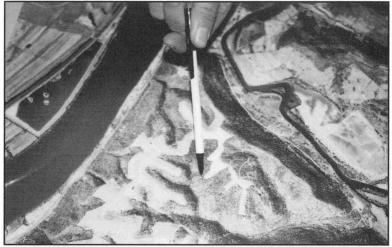

Never underestimate the value of an aerial photo to supplement your boots-on-the-ground scouting. From the air, patterns and terrain features that you might never see on the ground often become clear.

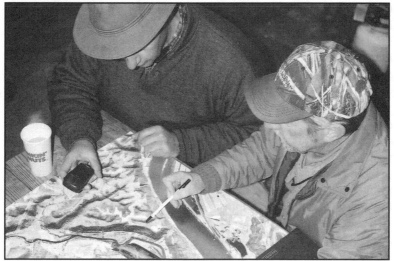

Use your on-the-ground snapshots to compare views with aerial photos. If you can sit down for a study with the landowner, you can quickly pinpoint good potential stand locations.

Maps of all kinds are useful, from topographic maps to soil types to weather maps and aerial photos, which are a kind of visual map. You would guess that if you are hunting a distant location, a wilderness area or a large wildlife management area, a map is obviously going to be beneficial in helping you locate potential deer bedding areas and routes of travel. But they are also useful in getting to know hunting locales in your own neighborhood. They can help you find the right place to park your truck for the wind conditions and maybe give you some clues about how best to enter and leave your area, making as little disturbance as possible. Combined with a weather service map of the prevailing winds, you will best be able to understand how your scent is going to disperse.

A note about aerial photos and photos in general. Your county agricultural extension agent or the US Department of Agriculture's Farm Service Agency will be able to direct you to aerial resources, but in my experience those on hand are at worst years and at very best many months old. In addition, the resolution may not be high enough to be beneficial. So, government aerials can be helpful, but you want to write history, not read about it. Plus, hanging around in these gray government offices with their filing cabinets, cautious clerks and bureaucrats is creepy.

An option is to rent a plane (and a pilot!) for a couple hours and take your own pictures. You are guaranteed that they will be timely and accurate. You will know precisely which road is being graded, and you will be able to get a much more expansive view of deer travel routes than from the ground. From the air, you can see linkages that on the ground would be invisible or would take you hours to understand. Of course, in my other life, I am a commercial airline pilot. So you may be thinking, "It's easy for him to say," but I find that people who own small charter services or even some kinds of open-cockpit planes are eager for a chance to pick up a fare or just to build up their hours flying if you will pay for a rental.

Be sure to discuss your objective with the pilot before you fly. The objective is to end up with very clear, permanent images of your hunting area, the kind you can print, enlarge and study over a cup of coffee before you make decisions about the area and go in on foot. You will not want to rent a plane on a hazy day because the haze or smoke will obscure your pictures. You will not want to fly early in the morning or late in the afternoon, as these times give you shadows that are difficult for the person who is not skilled in photo interpretation to factor. You do want to fly as slow as possible over your objective and this will mean leaning out of the airplane to take your pictures; the slower the better for the highest resolution photos. Study the safety harness system in the seat and be sure you can move to take pictures. You need the window open and for your best photo angle, the pilot will have to bank into a turn (fly at an angle), so if you get airsick or carsick easily, be sure you let the pilot know in advance. He or she will provide airsickness bags. Talk about these things in advance, and if your pilot seems more interested in being paid than in your best interests, go elsewhere. But expect to have fun.

Two considerations are the cost and the type of results you are going to get. If you split the cost with a buddy, it will be about the same as taking a couple guys to lunch in the city and even if you do not split the cost, how much is it worth to cut days off your investment in scouting for a big deer? Most small planes of the variety you will be able to charter will only be able to take one passenger who can shoot pictures, so if you split the cost with a hunting buddy, the closer he hunts to your location, the better. And remember that film is cheap compared to your time and the cost of renting the plane and pilot. Burn film, but shoot cautiously. There is nothing worse than coming down from a flight that cost a couple hundred dollars with four rolls of blurry, indecipherable film.

Speaking of film and cameras, what works best for aerial photos? Your home camera will do, but use a fast, high-quality film. Don't scrimp here and use the film that is on sale at the local BoxMart and then have your film processed at the local drug store. There is surely a professional film developer in your neighborhood, and I believe it is worthwhile to pay a few extra dollars for his service. Your family camera will work, but the better the quality camera, the better the optical lenses and mechanics. So, take the best camera you can beg or borrow and take a back-up. I know professional photographers and writers who salvaged an assignment when their Number 1 camera had a mechanical problem and they used the back-up.

Whether you choose to shoot digital or with film does not particularly matter. What matters is using a camera that gives you the best quality image possible. These days, you can direct link most digital cameras into a home computer and view your photos on screen, enlarging or printing the best ones as needed. With a digital and download ability, you can zoom to a particular field corner or zoom out to study the relationship of a brushy draw to the prevailing wind during the rut and your best approach to a stand at oh-dark-thirty in the morning. Then you can walk it.

You may need a lens filter or two on your camera to help cut through any haze or smoke that appears when you are in the air and to give you the best contrast possible in your ground images. A screw-on lens filter rearranges the light entering your camera. It automatically selects and rearranges some wavelengths and blocks others. Pull on your shooting glasses to understand this point. Glasses with yellow lenses make the world seem intensely brighter, but they flatten contrast. Glasses with red lenses heighten the contrast between color hues, brighten other colors and block out hazy blue.

Red is my choice for shooting glasses and for a lens filter, but when it comes to your camera, you need to find out if lens filters are available; and if so, what the cost will be. Filters are not designed for most of the family 35 mm cameras sold at local drug stores and BoxMarts, but your local

"I do not waste time looking for shed antlers," Tim says. "Shed hunting is fine if you are someplace other than your primary hunting spot, but I only want antlers when they are still attached to bucks like this."

specialty camera store will be able to suggest some options. (Another good reason to shop small and pay the few extra dollars required for personal service from professionals.)

Once you have selected the right site, you will begin to assemble data in preparation for putting your boots on the deer's turf. Remember why you are going to this extra trouble. Your chosen mission is to kill one of these deer, but not just any one of them, only the very finest specimen. So, make everything you do deliberate. Pursue that goal and no other.

Blackpowder hunters have some of the advantages of guns and some of the disadvantages of bows, like flat shooting over relatively short distances.

If your son or daughter wants to go hunting with you one afternoon, do not take them to your trophy spot. (In fact, the location you have chosen may be one you only want to share with your spouse and trusted hunting buddies. For your safety though, share it with someone!) Take your kids anywhere but the spot you've chosen to kill a trophy. For them, I suggest you find a place with lots of deer so they can see what it is all about. (Fishermen say their kids get hooked when the fish are biting, but if they have to sit in a boat all day without catching anything, their interest fades pretty fast.) If you have multiple tags, go ahead and take a deer for or with them. For their first deer or first few deer, every big-game animal is a trophy. Try to put yourself in their place. But to reiterate, in the location you have chosen to hunt mature bucks, take no one. Do not picnic there with your family. Do not drive around it casually on your way home from church on Sunday afternoon. Do not go to work and brag about the sign you see there. You have made a personal commitment that takes time, effort and costs money. That is valuable. Protect it. I say again, "No pressure!"

It is time to spread the aerial photos and topo information out on the kitchen table and study it all together. All the time you have been driving around the area and talking to landowners, you have been sketching maps and making notes. Now, before you head out into the field, is the right time to consolidate the information you have gathered and to make a working field map. Again, it doesn't have to be fancy. I am going to assume that you are not an artist. Your base map needs to show the area carefully, prevailing wind direction and specific terrain features. Remember that the purpose of a map is to make your actual hunting time easier and more productive, to fashion a tool. The map itself, pretty or ugly, is not the objective. You want to identify and mark seasonal food sources and probable bedding sites so that you can get into and out of the area as easily as possible and without unnecessarily disturbing the deer, especially that mature buck you are after. After you kill him, it will be okay to scream at the top of your lungs and blow the horn and wave all the way to the check station and taxidermist.

At this point, many writers suggest that you transect your hunting area, i.e. walk it in a grid pattern looking for deer sign. I think this idea is wrong. If you have gone to the trouble of interviewing area individuals, if you have studied available maps, perhaps flown over the area to take current photos and carefully noted the surroundings, you should have a darn good idea of what lies inside your zone of interest.

How would you walk a grid through the woods? Well, you can possibly walk a grid using a lensatic compass, recognizing that you cannot do it perfectly even on a flat, open parking lot much less in either the wilderness or over the broken terrain, blowdowns and thick vegetation of a relatively small woodlot.

What are you going to see by walking a grid? The writers who suggest this technique believe that you can totally understand your hunting area if you walk it completely and carefully observe what is going on around you. They say this allows you to systematically cover and understand your territory.

So, I have changed my mind. This idea of walking a grid over your hunting area is not just wrong, it is a bad idea. Here is why I think so. First, walking any grid is virtually impossible. You are going to spend as much time checking the compass and map as you do observing what is around you. Second, your boots are not equipped to tiptoe through the woods like a ninja. Take a tape recorder and fasten it below your belt, about the height of a deer's head. You will be surprised at the noise. We crash and thunder and knock over bushes and leave human scent everywhere we go.

If you do not think this is the case, try ghosting through the woods for a hundred yards. It is impossible. Or if you can go a hundred yards, your back is going to ache and your knees are going to complain and your senses are going to rebel. We have not been raised and adapted to a go-slow, be-careful world. We are not Tom Cruise in "The Last Samurai" and neither is Tom. We are not good at this stealth thing, this cat-like stalking with total body and mind control. We never have been good at it, and that's exactly

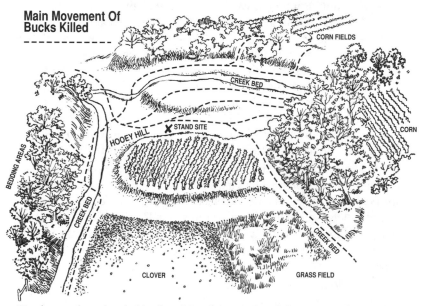

Tim has made such a habit of studying the ground and then moving his stand in response to weather conditions that this plot of ground in southern Ohio has become known as "Hooey Hill."

why making a commitment to take only mature deer is such a big challenge. Plus, deer may be meat on the hoof, but they are not stupid. What is the point of advertising your presence? They know you, your bacon and eggs and the gasoline on the soles of your boots are not natural in their environment; and if they are not natural, they are threatening. Wild, free-ranging deer are not going to become accustomed to you crashing around in their home. Transect the woods? Phooey.

So, when you do finally begin to put yourself in the deer woods, here are a few suggestions about what to do, what to wear and how to see what you are observing.

• Do not wear your hunting clothes or take your hunting gear. Save that stuff for hunting. It is tucked away securely in a plastic bag with a little earth scent wafer or some leaves. Do not unpack it to go scouting. While we are on the subject of equipment, you do not want to take practice shots or shoot at squirrels from the stand you are going to kill your trophy, and you do not want to hang a treestand your first time out, either. What is the point in making a commitment, going to a lot of trouble and then being careless and messing it up?

• While some deer hunters believe in putting up a stand and sitting on it during the "off months," I find that the times when I have followed that advice have not been productive. Plus, I have enough trouble being disciplined on stand without the added obstacle of knowing that I am just there to watch. And anyway, I like to get my "honey-do projects" finished off way before hunting season. I think of this as opening a savings account for my time in the woods. During the season, I actually do like to hoist a stand up a tree until I need oxygen and then sit in it to look over a wider circle of territory. This practice has at times let me see and track deer I would not otherwise have noticed, but at 35 feet in the air or higher, the shot angle becomes prohibitive for a broadhead-tipped arrow, so when I do this during the day, I do not consider it hunting; it's more like scouting.

• I waste no time looking for shed antlers, either. If I run across one or a set, fine. If not, who cares? It's a deer with a rack that I am dedicated to, not a rack without a deer attached or a deer without a rack. Sure, a nice set of shed antlers is proof that a big deer came by at least one time and that he may still be alive and roaming the area. On the other hand, he may not still be alive and only his offspring survive with his genetic potential, which, we hope, he has passed on to a number of receptive does.

• I would not go scouting without a knife, a little saw and some string. They are useful for a hundred tasks and in some emergencies, too. Eventually, as the land and the deer herd's distribution and movements become clear, I will want to select a stand site and perhaps very selectively trim or tie back a few branches in my shooting lanes. I am not a big believer in making wholesale changes to the woods before hunting them. Deer notice and the changes affect their movement. In the North, you will not see much foliage in the peak of the hunting season. With this in mind, I believe the best time for pressing the intended area of ambush should be in February and March. The ground will be devoid of leafy cover and deer will be in their post-breeding, wintering and yarding areas, not running around in the areas they inhabit when vegetation and natural foods are plentiful.

• Once I have found the best possible stand for delivering big deer into my shooting lanes, I want to prepare it and mark a trail in and out with some product like Fire Tacks that will be visible to me but obscure to other hunters. If I have worked hard to find the best spot to take a mature deer, I sure don't want other hunters following my trail or taking advantage of my not being on stand one day. This is why I don't use orange surveyor's tape to mark a trail. It is much too visible.

• Do carry a couple pencils, paper and a copy of your working map. I have found that taking an old fashioned clipboard and a pad of legal paper

Several fixed-position Gorilla stands are lightweight, safe and portable. In the past 10 years, manufacturers have worked hard to make them comfortable as well.

works for me. Carry a couple pencils because you are going to break the point on one and you will need a back-up. Take a pen, you say? Too messy and they do not come with erasers.

• Do take a set of binoculars. In the Eastern woods, they will not be of great use every day, but every now and then you will be glad you have them. Try to find a lightweight pair with the biggest field of view you can buy. Magnification is not nearly as important as field of view. And, while I adore expensive, fancy gear as much as the next guy, my experience says you do not have to spend a lot of money. There are some wonderful binoculars available and marketed to sportsmen at all price ranges, but the real expensive sets are overkill. A good, cheap set will usually work just fine in the Eastern states and these days most lenses are made in Japan or China.

• In the final stages of scouting, you want to take a rangefinder so that you can begin memorizing distances to landmarks. You do not want to practice shooting from your stand. Practice in your backyard. Learn distance estimation by walking the neighborhood and playing a guessing game with yourself. Once you get to your deer area though, concentrate, tread lightly and get in and out as quickly as you can with the information you want. Expensive laser rangefinders are accurate, but they have been

If you think taking big bucks on a consistent basis takes all of the stealth and patience you can summon, try accomplishing this with a cameraman and all of his gear in a tree next to you. Tim often hunts with his friend Terry Rohm (right) of Tink's.

over-promoted, unless you live in the West where you can see and shoot for hundreds of yards. A coincident rangefinder, which works without batteries (Imagine that!) by simply superimposing two images, will give bowhunters distance estimation readings that quickly fall within our shooting capabilities. In other words, a coincident rangefinder's +/- 1 yard shooting error at 30 yards is still better than most of us can consistently estimate from an elevated stand when a big buck is in our sights. Sad, but true. The reason is to make note of potential trees in which to hang a stand. You will want to make note of any tree that positions you downwind, between 20 and 30 yards of where you expect to see deer moving.

• Take a camera. Not so much for scouting, although I like to make a record of the scrapes and rubs and any other stuff that catches my eye, but because nothing is better than a photo with notes on the back. Today, a reasonably priced camera with a zoom lens that takes good pictures will fit in your back pocket. If you do find a tree you think might be suitable, take a few pictures from ground level. This will give you a ground perspective that can help you determine whether additional cover is needed as well as the height requirement for your stand.

• I like these new trail cameras, by the way. They cost a couple hundred bucks for a good one with infrared activation, a camouflaged waterproof case and time sequencing, and they will give you some surprising snapshots. I do not think we really know yet how they affect big deer, whether they spook them or cause them to change their habits. I do know what a blinding flash would do to me if it went off in my face in the middle of a dark night after I had left my stand, however.

• Be safe. Leave your spouse a note and a map of where you will be. Do not just tell her (that will not stand up later in court). If you have a cell phone, take it with you.

• While we are on the subject, take water, an energy bar or two, a whistle and a disposable pocket flashlight. All this stuff will fit into a cheap day pack with your camera and rangefinder. Nobody ever expects to fall and break a leg or have a heart attack in the woods, but it happens dozens of times each year. You want the big deer? Be smart. Be safe when you go into the woods.

Remember that you are scouting for big deer, mature deer. The key to locating these deer is to find their travel routes, back and forth from their preferred bedding areas to food. This leads you along trails to the intersection of specific terrain features like ridges, fencerows, natural or man-made funnels or deep agricultural ditches. You are not scouting for their rubs or for scrapes or even fresh droppings or tracks. These things indicate that deer are present, but they are only temporary substitutes for the real thing. On the other hand, if an area remains relatively undisturbed from one year to the next, deer will select the same basic locations to rub their antlers and to make scrapes. So, jot these things down on your map as indicative of deer activity or travel routes and then go look for more important sign or terrain features like a natural deer funnel or the points where a brushy fencerow enters the woods.

Here, Tim asks Dr. Karl Miller from the University of Georgia about a subject every deer hunter wants to know more about – rubs and scrapes and their importance in creating a successful hunting strategy. Dr. Miller's answers may surprise you!

Rubs and Scrapes

Tim: In the last few years, speculation among hunters has led to dismissing rubs as little more than a buck scraping the velvet off his antlers. Would you say this is correct?

Dr. Miller: Not at all. There is good research and structured observation indicating that rubs are important indicators of the number, age and sex structure of deer in an area.

Due to photoperiodism and rising testosterone levels in bucks before the rut, the velvet falls off. Also, Tom Atkeson and Jon Gassett have documented that the apocrine and sebaceous (forehead) glands between a buck's antlers become active in the fall. These glands produce a complex and apparently "personal" chemical signature. We think bucks can actually identify one another by licking the chemicals deposited on a rub.

Studying various locations, Larry Marchinton and I found that dominant older bucks make many more rubs than younger, sub-dominant bucks. On average, a buck may make anywhere from about 400 to 800 rubs in a season and the more dominant a buck is, the earlier it starts. If the dominant buck isn't harvested, he will continue rubbing right up to the peak of the rut.

Tim: Amazing! This means effective scouting is more important than ever.

Dr. Miller: That's right. In Michigan, John Ozoga found that the number of rubs is directly related to the density of older bucks, and here in Georgia, we find that food availability is a big factor as well.

Think of rubs this way. A rub not only helps bucks communicate with each other, but it is a communication device for hunters, too. If you hunt an area with a lot of fresh rubs, you can draw several tentative conclusions: there are just a lot of bucks in the area

Bucks rub an amazing number of times, and a variety of glands deposit individual scents on rubbed trees. Hunting buddy Henry Rockey inspects a big rub in Ohio.

or there are just a few bucks that are highly concentrated or there are some mature dominant bucks present, the kind you want to hunt. Pre-season scouting helps you understand the age structure because mature bucks rub earlier and more frequently, maybe making as many as 1000 rubs during the 90-day period from September until December. It could be that making a rub is like a dog peeing around the yard. He's saying this is his territory, and he's the big dog in the yard.

Tim: How do rubs and scrapes relate to one another?

Dr. Miller: We have studied scrapes for many years but are only now beginning to understand them. Unlike rubs that involve only scent from the forehead glands, a scrape involves several scent sources and apparently has multiple tasks in deer communication, recognition and reproduction.

All evidence and observation indicates that bucks make scrapes, and it is generally bucks that visit them; but scrapes are like calling cards for does, too. The mixture of chemicals in a scrape may have a role in synchronizing the rut so that fawns are born and grow up at about the same time of the year.

It is older, more dominant bucks in the 2 1/2-year-and-older age group that make most of the scrapes. They begin with an overhanging branch and seem to mark it with a variety of chemicals and scents from glands in their forehead, glands around the eyes and nose and even saliva. Then they paw away the leaves underneath and urinate over their tarsal glands while rubbing them vigorously together. This probably deposits odors from the tarsals and even from the interdigital glands between their toes. As a result, a lot of chemical information is concentrated in a small spot, and we think it becomes communication when visited by other deer.

Based on studies by John Ozoga, Karen Alexy and Jon Gassett, it appears that most scrapes appear 2 to 3 weeks before the rut kicks off. In fact, the appearance of scrapes is a sign that the rut is beginning. Once the rut begins, scrape visitation drops to almost zero.

Tim: So, would you recommend hunting over a scrape?

Dr. Miller: No. Motion-activated video cameras indicate that almost 90 percent of scrape visits occur at night.

Kneeling beneath a hanging overhead branch, Tim studies the relationship of two fresh scrapes to the general direction of deer travel in his Michigan "honey hole."

Number 5 –
Use The Record Books With Caution

Record books. Some hunters live and die by what they read in the columns and printed analyses of statistics in books produced by the Pope & Young Club and the Boone & Crockett Club and, to a lesser extent, the Safari Club International and the Buckmasters full-credit scoring system. Some people live and die by these clubs ... but most do not.

The North American records clubs were organized to keep statistics about certain kinds of trophy animals. This they do relatively well. They

Table 1: Whitetail Bucks Scored and Entered in the Pope & Young and Boone & Crockett Record Books by State

State	P&Y Typical	P&Y Non-Typical	B&C Typical & Non-Typical	Totals
Wisconsin	3,277	149	377	3,803
Illinois	2,633	212	363	3,208
Iowa	1,541	139	455	2,135
Minnesota	1,266	96	497	1,859
Ohio	1,159	86	161	1,406
Kansas	984	125	178	1,287
Michigan	739	0	107	846
Missouri	675	40	181	896
Indiana	619	32	93	744
Texas	596	21	242	859
New York	441	16	39	496
Maryland	392	18	35	445
Kentucky	390	25	167	582
Pennsylvania	373	9	25	407
Nebraska	349	30	96	475
South Dakota	294	14	78	386
Oklahoma	255	17	41	313
Montana	252	11	93	356
New Jersey	221	4	1	226
North Dakota	219	8	40	267
Virginia	195	8	45	248
West Virginia	186	7	9	202

also serve as a social nexus for the men and women who hunt specifically for "the book." It is interesting to consult these records, and if you are the kind of person who likes numbers, who likes to study lists and comparisons of charts and graphs, or who has plenty of cash to travel across the U.S. to hunt, you can have a whale of a time with the information these clubs generate.

Is the information these clubs generate accurate, sufficient and complete? This is a complex question. Many people who take a mature buck choose not to register it with one of the clubs or they simply do not care enough about the clubs and their functions to choose one way or the other.

State	P&Y Typical	P&Y Non-Typical	B&C Typical & Non-Typical	Totals
Mississippi	144	2	41	187
Georgia	143	6	83	232
Arkansas	128	11	85	214
Colorado	105	5	19	129
Alabama	90	3	13	106
Tennessee	84	3	20	107
Massachusetts	79	1	4	84
Connecticut	77	2	5	84
North Carolina	74	2	8	84
Louisiana	61	1	35	97
Washington	55	5	38	98
Wyoming	44	1	27	72
Idaho	41	2	39	82
New Hampshire	38	0	14	52
Delaware	30	0	6	36
Maine	21	1	73	95
South Carolina	19	0	4	23
Rhode Island	8	0	0	8
Florida	7	0	1	8
Oregon	7	2	3	12
Vermont	4	0	3	7
TOTAL	18,315	1,114	3,844	23,263

The reasons for registering and scoring a trophy or not are various and personal. They range from sheer vanity to the desire to be part of a national organization whose secondary objective (after that of keeping good records) is to preserve and promote hunting. However, there are no statistics that tell us what percentage of trophy deer killed are registered or whether the deer that are scored and registered are at all biologically representative of herd dynamics. So, whether or not these trophy records are complete is not a question we will ever be able to address, although we know that in certain instances, senior members of the clubs have voted to delete the records of convicted felons (rather than just deleting the hunter's name). We know that for the information supplied, the books are relatively complete. Are they complete enough to base your travel and hunting decisions? I, for one, don't think so unless the area you identify is close and in this case, you have already done the scouting and interviewing to identify it.

Are the record books accurate? Well, they are based on information supplied by hunters and there is no reason to believe that this information is not true and accurate except for the suspicion that not every hunter, like not every fisherman – even those who attest to the truthfulness of the data – wants to divulge the location of their honey hole. So, my guess is that these books are accurate, as far as they go. Not a good answer, but it does help keep the data in perspective.

From even a quick perusal of record book lists, however, you can quickly identify which states and areas have more trophy deer registered. You will see that David S. Krempasky's 1985 non-typical whopper (190 2/8) was taken in Montgomery County, Pennsylvania, and that Bernard J. Crescione hauled a typical buck with a score of 155 4/8 out of Westchester County, New York, in 1960. Around the turn of the century, the 21st century that is, the states with most deer scored and registered were Wisconsin, Illinois, Iowa, Minnesota, Ohio, Kansas, Michigan, Missouri, Indiana, and Texas; and the Canadian prairie provinces of Manitoba and Alberta are well represented. So, big deer come out of the heartland in great numbers and this is about where the greatest concentration of hunters lives, too. They are by and large the states you read about in the popular hunting magazines. I believe you already know where big deer are killed and you don't need record books to tell you.

What you may overlook when you are too focused on the big numbers put up by corn-fed states in the heartland is that really big, mature deer come out of your state, too. There's Logan County, Colorado (1981), and Lewis County, Kentucky (1985). And what about St. Mary's County, Louisiana (1981), Sullivan County, Tennessee (1984), Opelika, Alabama (1980), Amherst County, Virginia (1980) or Kent County, Maryland (1962)!

I have two points to make. First, the point that we have made over and over in this book is that big, mature deer live practically everywhere there are deer, probably in your own neighborhood. Second, unless you just happen to like doing it, spending hours poring over the national record books can easily mislead you.

By the time you buy your record book and begin plotting a strategy to find big deer, both the book and its entries will be history. Are you interested in reading history or making history? Do you really care about entries from the 1950s or even the 1990s? Of course, they establish a pattern over time, but is it a pattern that surprises you? Not if you attend any hunting seminars or read – even occasionally – a hunting magazine. The environment in a rapidly growing America with 300 million human inhabitants is dynamic. It changes and the Zen people tell us that it changes every day. We struggle to find a place for wildlife in a rapidly growing, paved-over urbanizing nation. We struggle with political issues such as deer hunting on the Shiawassee National Wildlife Refuge in Michigan, which has produced numerous trophy bucks. Even though the recording clubs make an effort to keep up-to-date data in the pipeline, the record books are essentially static while the situation on the ground is fluid.

Besides, say you live in Pennsylvania and have made a commitment to hunt for and take only mature deer. You are frustrated that you cannot seem to locate big bucks within driving distance of your home. So, you book a hunt in Pike County, Illinois – a spot that is getting a lot of current attention – and pay $2500 plus expenses to hunt at a lodge there for 5 days. You know in advance that taking a trophy away from home is like winning the lottery. You will not win if you don't purchase a ticket, but even before

Tim's cameraman studies a high-quality "edge" with a planted field, food plot and brushy margin. This looks like an excellent spot to set up for deer.

you buy the ticket, you know that the odds are a hundred-million-to-one that you will actually take home a really big buck. Paying one dollar for a lottery ticket is one thing. Paying $2500 for a lottery ticket is something else. Even after you arrive at a lodge and look at all the pictures on the wall of hunters with giant deer, do you realistically expect that your picture will be up there one day? You must have confidence in yourself, not in the million-to-one possibility.

I am not saying that you should not hunt anywhere except home. I am saying that you need to control your expectations, not let them control you. You want to budget your resources (time, money, energy) wisely.

The first thing I am going to tell you about hunting with an outfitter is the ultimate in truths. You are only going to be as good as he is. You are buying his knowledge and skills as a hunter. He picks the area, the stand … the whole game plan. He is the horse you are betting on, and you better have this mind-set going in.

On the other hand, I have been to some good places and hunted with some excellent outfitters, people who simply know the game and their area inside and out. It absolutely drives me crazy to see a client who, through ignorance or because things are not going his way, throws a temper tantrum during a hunt. It happens and it is sad.

When you work with an outfitter, you must be aware that there are things that are totally out of his control: storms, high winds, spikes up or down in temperature, international events and so on. A serious hunter needs to be prepared, to have the right gear and the right mind-set.

This is one of the reasons I rarely hunt with an outfitter. I want to control where I put my boots on the ground and what direction I want to face. I am selfish that way (and I want you to be that way, too). I want to hunt when and where I determine it is best to take a mature deer. Nothing else will do.

I have had wonderful experiences with outfitters, though, in particular, the Midwesterners Steve Shoop and Mike White. Both are top-shelf operators.

If you pay big dollars and go to a lodge in an area that has, in the past, produced big bucks, you should not define the success of your experience by whether you haul a giant home in your trunk or not. That may be your objective and it can certainly happen, but an overwhelming number of hunters who travel to a lodge take home nothing at all or a deer that does not make the record books. Normally, a lodge encourages its customers to help them take does off the property. In current wildlife theory, killing does strengthens the deer herd, and for bowhunters especially, who typically have success rates of 10 to 15 to maybe 20 percent annually, taking a doe gives us some sense of fulfillment, puts some expensive meat on the table.

An 8-point that may or may not satisfy your hunting goals is, nevertheless, a trophy when taken with a bow.

You have to go on an expensive lodge trip as if you were taking a trip to Las Vegas. This is the right mind-set: I am going to do my best, but it is not going to be the end of the world if I leave my money in the hands of the blackjack dealer. In most cases, the deer and the dealer have the odds on their side. The goal is to maximize my potential, not be the poor sap that loses his paycheck to the house every year. The alternative is this: If you define the success of an exotic hunting experience as seeing a new place, hanging out with a bunch of other hunters, learning some new hunting tactics and having someone else cater your meals and clean up after you for five days, then you probably will not be disappointed. You will have fun and your money will be well spent.

I totally believe that your best odds for a really big deer are hunting right at home where you can intensively study the area and work hard to make your commitment come to fruition. If you could just pay $2500 and be assured of a trophy, it would diminish the accomplishment. Unless you get extremely lucky at a place you lease in Kansas or a lodge you visit, your mission is to do the work so that you don't have to "get lucky." You want to do the work to be assured of success, to be the best you can be.

I am not anti-record books or record-keeping clubs. I choose not to register trophy deer, but that is strictly a personal decision. My motivation for hunting only mature-class bucks is internal. To quote a current car advertisement, I am "driven by what's inside" rather than the opinions of others or the standards of a private club. So, my estimation of and enjoyment of what I do, right or wrong, well or poorly, is completely up to me to decide.

I believe that clubs like Boone & Crockett and Pope & Young are beneficial because they call us to a higher standard. They organize to raise funds to combat anti-hunter terrorism and to promote wildlife restoration and conservation projects. These clubs help with the vital missions of education and information. Seeing my name in a record book, however, is not the reason I hunt and not the reason I have made a commitment to take only mature deer. Besides, because I often shoot a compound bow with a let-off higher than 65 percent, P&Y has grudgingly agreed to enter the trophy … with an asterisk! Very generous indeed.

To find a more useful set of data than the national statistics, locate your relevant state organization. In Ohio, for example, the Buckeye Big Buck Club has long been recognized as a strong organization for hunters with credible trophy data. Ohio's Division of Wildlife's annual hunting regulations contain a map of the state superimposed with the 2002-03 deer harvest and a summary of the 1958-2003 trophy deer registered by county by the Big Buck Club. Interestingly, trophy bucks have been registered in every county in that state. Most states have similar grass-roots organizations, which moves you one practical step closer to your goal.

Using local data moves you closer to your goal, but how far will you be willing to travel each time you want to go hunting? The simple answer is, "As far as it takes." This is a key question for your hunting success, however, and the essential problem with the national records. They are very interesting, but are they any more practically useful to you than a newspaper or magazine article about a state deer hunting hotspot? Figure that by the time an area becomes a legitimate hotspot, everyone in the local area already knows about it. By the time a professional writer collects the data, does the interviews, assembles the information into a good story, sells it to a magazine, the magazine publishes the story and you read it, the area was a hotspot a year ago at best.

So, how far will you go? If you believe that big, mature deer live practically everywhere there are deer – sure, more in some areas than others – you should not have to drive very far. If, on the other hand, you buy into the theory that big deer only live and are more easily harvested in certain pockets of the US (west-central Illinois, for instance), you better buckle up. The farther your hunting area from where you live, the more difficult it becomes to get there and the less frequently you will hunt. So, it is a matter of odds. If you are convinced that one trip is all you need, then you should go for it, wherever your inclination leads. If you believe that we are hunters rather than killers and that we call it hunting for a reason – because we fail to see and/or connect with a trophy on most trips to the field – closer is certainly better.

Let's say that you decide to travel to some well-publicized "trophy area" and look for a place to hunt. Chances are that unless you have relatives there, you will have to lease the land. How long you want to hunt there and perhaps what time of year you want to be there – one trip or a week early in the season before the bucks become spooked or during the peak of the rut – will depend on how much it is going to cost.

Landowners, and especially farmers and ranchers, have become savvy about their property. They understand that they control access to a valuable resource, and given the uncertain prices they receive for crops and cattle, they need the sportsman's dollars to help pay their taxes. This is an unfortunate trend and bodes for a potentially dark future for our children, but you can appreciate their position. In a good area, a hundred guys a year will knock on their door and ask if they can hunt their land.

And do not even think you can find a hotspot without going there in person unless you answer an ad in a state or regional paper, in which case you are going to have to pay. Expect to meet landowners face-to-face. If you have to, take out an advertisement in the local newspapers:

Responsible bowhunter seeks land to lease for whitetail deer hunting. Willing to sign a liability waiver upon receipt of written lease.

Do not forget the release of liability. Do not forget your telephone number. And do not forget that you are not interested in just any deer.

If you do lease property that is distant from your home, the complications compound, but the same scouting rules apply. Scout harder to make your hunting easier.

Chapter 8

Discover The Topographic Advantages

Can you determine trends in deer movement? Absolutely. And this is where you transition to a truly accomplished deer hunter. This is vitally important for the hunter who wants to kill mature whitetails. For many years I have been conducting seminars on the subject, and I often use past hunting experiences as examples of how to effectively use topographic interpretation to identify key locations. At one of them, within about two hours, I saw nine bucks pass within bow range. Several people who have heard me tell the story told me I was lucky. Maybe. I believe in luck or coincidence or divine intervention or whatever you want to call it when things just seem to fall into place. I also believe that you can make your own luck, can stack the cards in your favor.

Whether you are hunting near home or in a place in which you are not too familiar, I want you to make your own luck by finding a topographic advantage. There are seven topographic elements or irregularities that will help you connect with all of the needs of the whitetail (food, water, secure bedding areas and travel routes). Those elements are funnels, corners, natural shelves, logging roads, low spots, ridge ramps and what I call "spider webs." Using a topographic advantage, I find hot stand setups 95 percent of the time. I don't claim that I always kill a big deer with that magnificent frequency, but I do place myself in position to do so.

"Spider Webs"

Thousands of eyewitness accounts from successful hunters tell us that whitetails prefer to travel sheltered routes between their bedding and feeding areas. It is my experience that the deeper and more densely packed with brush is a fencerow or ditch, the more heavily traveled it will be. A "spider web" is a location where two or more ditches or fencerows intersect. If you can situate a blind or stand near multiple spider webs, your chances of seeing plenty of deer are terrific.

The key to locating these spider webs lies in using all your tools to scout intersecting travel routes. (How close these routes run to area roads is also a factor as close proximity encourages unethical and trespassing road hunters.) The arms of the spider web need to connect to or else help the deer move quietly and unseen toward woodlots and abandoned homesteads for bedding, or fields or orchards that serve as back-up food sources. It helps if there is a variety of brushy undergrowth for cover. This gives deer a sense of security, a feeling that they can move around without being continually harassed by predators. When I began searching for effective stand and ground blind locations based on topographic advantages like spider webs, the percentage of time I saw quality deer went up dramatically.

Funnels

I admit being partial to hunting funnels. Think of a funnel as a natural or even a man-made topographic element that predetermines deer travel routes. A traditional forest funnel can be a ravine or a swath of timber, which decreases in width to a bottleneck or hourglass shape. Couple a fun-

A rub line followed this ridge from a small agricultural field to a high sheltered cove where deer were bedding.

nel with terrain that is difficult to negotiate or have a funnel that interrupts what would otherwise be an easy path to and from a food source and you have an ideal spot to kill a big deer. You often find man-made funnels in or between fields and woodlots with intersecting ditches and fencerows, places where fields narrow or widen dramatically. These are all predictable zones for deer travel.

You can make your own funnel of course, and then position your stand to take advantage of its channeling effect, if you start well in advance of the season so that deer will become accustomed to it as part of their normal environment. I know successful hunters who have used the portable snow fencing commonly used by many road departments to alter deer movement into their shooting lanes. Such a pro-active move depends on the terrain and its relationship to local bedding and feeding areas.

Although deer have no fear of getting their feet wet, observation has shown me, that given the option, most will take a dry route and skirt around rivers, creeks, sloughs, swamps and just about any sizeable body of water. The deeper the water is, the wider the deer highway around it. The ground around the waterline tends to provide sufficient cover as well as an abundant supply of mast. Anyone who has ever had the chance to hunt in the southern part of the country, particularly Alabama, Mississippi or Louisiana, will attest to this fact. One of my favorite hotspots is a funnel formed by a river and a housing development on the edge of a small town. The key here is to be aware that anything that conditions the direction of movement, even man-made obstacles or human activity, can and will cause the funneling effect.

Field Edges

Field edges are important for seeing deer, but they can be tough to hunt. My theory is that older whitetails usually enter open fields from the corners … and at night. Upon its entrance from a corner or even before, an animal can view the entire area quickly rather than being forced to search for danger in all directions, thus always leaving one of its flanks unprotected.

What makes field edges hard to hunt for mature deer is the difficulty of positioning yourself to intercept them. I have hunted planted fields and food plots many times and see deer enter the fields at all times of day. It is not unusual to see antlerless deer standing in the middle of the field at high noon. It is unusual to see a big, mature, antlered buck in the field at any time though, morning or evening. These big fellows tend to hang back in the timber and wait for dark before they move out to shadow the does, fawns and younger bucks.

The mechanics of shooting a bow have changed with the increasing sophistication of equipment. Tim believes in technology, but he is a deer freak, not a techno freak. "My only objective is to assemble shooting gear that will help me harvest mature bucks every year," he says.

When he is at full draw on a deer Tim says there are only three things on his mind: relax, pick a spot and kill this deer.

A former football player and current pilot for North-west Airlines, Tim balances his "time off" between family, producing a television show and his passion for hunting big deer.

The purpose of deer plantings is not just to harvest big deer, Tim says. The purpose of wildlife planting is to build the health of the herd. A healthy herd will naturally produce larger deer.

Ah, the old days! Tim swears that the trousers belonged to his dad.

Every whitetail hunter who prides himself on his ability to scout effectively, read sign and make decisions about deer movement is eventually faced with one decision: "Where should I hang a treestand to maximize my time in the field?" Tim solves that question by putting up multiple stands so that he can quickly make a decision about where to hunt based on the prevailing wind.

Tim believes that the principles for developing superior whitetail herds have been well worked out and are now becoming wide spread. This deer was killed on southern Ohio acreage that Tim helps manage exclusively for big bucks.

The essentials of Tim's positive and assertive message about man the predator, about making a commitment to do something that does not come easily and then sticking to it, apply equally to gun hunters and bowhunters.

Wearing his Scent-Lok activated-carbon suit including the hood over his nose and mouth, Tim gets aggressive and rattles for deer.

Tim's son Sean with his first deer. Young people need to learn hunting discipline with love and a view to success. Show them a little success and you will have a hunting partner forever.

Once Tim made a commitment to harvest mature deer, he found that he was working harder to make his dream happen, but eventually the results paid off in big deer!

Deer hair in the barbed wire is a sign that the observant hunter should not overlook. Positioning your stand back in the timber at least 50 yards from a deer crossing should result in consistent deer sightings.

Intensity and versatility are hallmarks of Tim's hunting style. If there are no trees for a stand, he might dig a pit blind or even set up in the tall grass. "I do whatever it takes," Tim says.

It is not unusual to see deer moving along ridges and shelves such as this one that is in full view of a nearby home in southern Ohio.

Your best play is to back off and locate a feature that allows you to nail them before they get to the field. Regardless, I have known big mature deer to be killed on fields. The most important factor you will have to deal with when making the choice of hunting on or near a field is the pressure factor. Unless you can be stealthy going to and from the location, as well as on stand, your presence will be felt and eventually pressure the deer out of the area and off the field.

The Effects of Gravity

Hilly country forces us to deal with the effects of gravity. Not only will you need to compensate for the trajectory of your arrow or bullet, but also you need to be aware of the effects of wind, water and human interference in the landscape. Natural shelves can occur along the sides of a ridge, and while I have some minor experience hunting shelves, I know several hunters who insist that mature animals frequently move along them to avoid the dangers of traveling with a higher profile.

Erosion at the bends and corners of a ridge creates natural ramps. These ramps, which connect different terrain features, make travel less difficult for deer and this enhances their usefulness as corridors and, therefore, as ambush sites.

Logging Roads

My experience with whitetails convinces me that they are lazy by nature. They often take the least restrictive route of travel when hunting pressure allows it. To make movement easier, deer use old logging roads or USDA Forest Service roads that are sometimes closed to public vehicles and thus become overgrown with weed and brush, ideal for browsing on a deer's way to and from primary food sources. Logging roads are excellent places to locate active scrapes during the rut, too.

My rule of thumb is the older, the better. In many areas, most of the timber is third- and fourth-generation forest. This timber is dominant in the Northeast (Pennsylvania and New York). Much of that area used to be small farms, but it has since been reclaimed by Appalachian hardwoods interspersed with stands of hemlock, white birch, cedar and pine. Some of the old roads have long been grown-over. This makes for excellent edge habitat and provides paths of least resistance through the woods. Laurel, bayberry and thick underbrush favor and soon reclaim these former openings.

Offered a choice of following an old switchback or climbing a steep Appalachian mountain ridge, deer will almost always use these old roads. Often old switchbacks, by design, connected one bench to another as they worked their way up mountain ridges, ridges that typically go for miles. A long mountain ridge will often have a saddle at the top where old roads cross and those saddles are great places to intercept bucks.

Old logging roads are terrific places to ambush big bucks, which, Tim believes, are extremely cautious but lazy by nature.

If you are hunting with a firearm, look for locations with an unobstructed shot. Unfortunately, the gun deer season can be a war zone, but you can use this to your advantage as deer use logging roads for escape routes. The higher switchbacks are used for cover with the deer skirting below ridgelines. The saddles are also opening-day hotspots as deer use these heavily to hightail-it from one side of a ridge to another. Opening-day pressure makes deer move – period.

Streambeds follow natural terrain features and intersect with ridges, fence lines and irrigation ditches. Deer do not hesitate to cross these streams by day or night. They also provide an excellent means of travel to and from your hunting locations.

One difficulty with logging roads, for hunters as well as for deer, is traveling along them undetected. A deer needs the freedom of movement to his bedding and primary food sources while a hunter needs to slip quietly into and out of his stand. This is especially critical when you have made a commitment to kill only mature game animals.

Low-Lying Areas

Too little has been written about the benefits of hunting low-lying areas for big deer. Low spots are excellent places for deer to bed or feed. One farm that I hunt has a 100-acre field with a portion in the eastern half that drops in elevation by about five feet. To avoid detection, deer feed heavily in this low spot, preferring it to the upper and more visible field. From the western edge of the field, they can't be seen, especially in low light situations.

Big-Woods Setups

Unless you are local or can scout thoroughly from a distance, states such as Pennsylvania, Kentucky, Maine, Missouri, New York and Ohio may present you with the greatest challenge for locating a successful stand setup. These "big-woods" states force hunters into the middle of huge, second-growth forests. This can be frustrating because in a large forested area, it can be difficult to come to grips with topographical advantages and clearly identify deer travel routes, bedrooms and primary feeding sources.

In Muy Grande Buck country in Texas' version of the big woods, much hunting is done on tripods from which some view of the country is granted. Bowhunters will feel naked on a tripod and will want to consider the pros and cons of a more restricted view with greater concealment by hunting from a ground blind.

Quality scouting and working to secure access to private property in the "off season" may be the long-range answer here.

In big-woods areas characterized by rolling and broken terrain like you find near the Appalachian Mountains and the Ohio River Valley, I stick to ridgetops, saddles and fingers of land. I carefully watch for sign that indicates deer travel running parallel to the ridges along such features as natural benches and shelves.

Saddles, or the low points between connecting points of higher ground, provide travel route hotspots for deer. After discovering a saddle, I try to set up on the ridge overlooking it. Because deer travel from one ridge to another, I'm careful not to set up in the middle of the saddle. These middle-of-the-saddle setups place the hunter in plain view of approaching deer, so you have to erect your ambush site 20 to 30 yards off the beaten path.

Another big-woods stand setup I like uses what I call "ridge ramps." In October 1999, I was hunting in southern Ohio with Ryan Klesko of the Atlanta Braves. I scouted an area where several ridge ramps or fingers of land met to form a low spot. I set up on one of the slightly elevated fingers of land running perpendicular to a nearby cornfield. Of all the spots available, this particular one had the most gradual slope.

At first light, I granted amnesty to a passing doe, her fawn and a small buck. Moments later, another small buck passed, its nose to the ground and on the trail of that doe, which was apparently coming into heat. Then, out of nowhere a mature 9-point appeared, running the same trail. The buck was heading down and across the ridge ramp en route to my location. His descent was going to place us almost eyeball-to-eyeball. I froze when he arrived on the upper trail. A favorable wind, a recharged Scent-Loc suit and head-to-toe Advantage camouflage with just a touch of Tink's Odor-Lok allowed me to remain completely hidden, even when he stopped and stared right through me toward the nearby cornfield.

The big buck stopped and browsed for a moment, apparently carefree, until he reached my entrance trail. Then he began the nervous body language typical of any whitetail that has detected human odor at what it must realize is close range. The buck slowly started back in the direction he came from, but it was uncertain. After what seemed like an eternity, the massive 9-point apparently made up its mind and turned back toward the field. I had begun to draw my Mathews Conquest when the buck glanced up, freezing me halfway through the draw. I held until I shook. Then, so slowly it seemed that he must have been toying with me, the buck lowered its head and stepped forward, placing its head behind a tree at about 35 yards. I horsed the bow back to full draw where I was only holding 25 pounds, and the moment he stepped out from the tree, I placed a broadhead through both of his lungs. I heard him collapse on the run after a 100-yard sprint.

I was doubly thrilled with that fine, 9-point buck. First, I patted myself on the back for scouting a new location and making a good decision about where to set up. Second, I had held that 70-pound Mathews bow halfway up the draw-force curve as long as I needed to and then made a killing shot. Since then, my good friend Lou Haubner renamed that sloping ridge ramp "Hooey Hill." It has produced five mature bucks in as many years, along with a lot of great memories.

Generally, terrain dictates the movement patterns of an area's whitetails. If you have made a commitment to take only mature animals, you must try to figure out where they are bedded. Unless they are disturbed or the rut is on, big deer stick close to the bedroom during daylight hours. These beds are usually located in the densest, most secluded terrain and brushy cover. Nevertheless, you would be surprised at how little cover it actually takes to make a whitetail almost invisible to the human eye.

A stand on a hillside will give you a good view through the late fall and winter woods, especially when you have a pair of binoculars in your field pack.

Here is a statistic that emphasizes what you need to do, tactically speaking, to score on a big deer. Ninety percent of all whitetails are killed within 1/4-mile of an easily accessible roadway. That's not the end of the story, though. Of these deer, 94 percent are does and yearlings. The bottom line is that big bucks require seclusion.

I am not one to barge into a bedding area to erect a stand. Deer bedrooms need to be handled with great care, or you will interrupt their patterns of movement, and all that will come of that is to make your work twice as hard. When they are run out of their bedding areas, deer will simply move to another home range.

If you just have to hunt a bedding area, do yourself a favor and select and erect your stand at night when deer are up and out feeding. Second, and this should be common sense, never enter the bedding area and climb into a stand when deer are present. You will get busted, and the spot will go dry immediately.

Rather than hunt in a bedding area, I prefer to hunt as close to its perimeter as possible without alerting the deer. Usually, the border of the bedding area in the direction of the primary food source presents the best opportunity for harvest. I look for this kind of spot, where two types of terrain meet to form a distinctive natural edge, as a "transition zone."

In the fall of 1998, I hunted Wisconsin and remember questioning the landowner about natural foods and the thickest woods. He told me that deer traveled from dense cover on the northwest corner of the property to a field that had been planted in nutrient-rich clover on the southeast portion of the ground. Between the two, an old logging road accessed the edge of what was now a tag alder swamp.

The swamp lay on the northern edge of some big timber between it and the remains of the succulent clover. Deer were bedding in the swamp where it was tangled and wet. In winter, the swamp froze over, filled with snow and gave them the additional protection of hearing the crunching snow from any approach. There was no snow on the ground when I was there. In the swamp and timber, the deer browsed on beechnut and a plentiful acorn crop while traveling the transition zone to and from the clover field. There were some decent rubs along the edge of the swamp, but no clues testified to the presence of trophy deer. Still, I felt that the swamp's secluded location had to offer sanctuary to a few fine bucks and that I could quickly locate deer moving in and out of the swamp. I positioned an API climbing stand 20 yards off the edge in the timber. Otherwise, I left the area completely undisturbed and did not cut as much as a twig for a shooting lane. This late in the season, I reasoned, cutting branches for shooting lanes would defeat the purpose of remaining undetected.

My first day on stand, I only saw a group of does. The second day, a spike wandered around nearby. I had expected more activity and was losing faith in my ability to choose a spot. By 10:00 in the morning of day three, the situation seemed bleak. All I could do was talk myself into staying confident.

"I know how to do this," I said to myself. "I am good at it. I have chosen the right spot. Relax. Be patient."

Then, I caught movement along the edge of the swamp. A really massive 10-pointer was walking along slowly in my direction. He stopped frequently to nose through the duff on the forest floor, probably looking for acorns. Obviously, he was headed back to his bedroom after a night out. Each time he stopped, he would cautiously look around, check the wind and rotate his ears in an effort to detect the slightest hint of danger. I drew my bow and whistled lightly. The buck froze and I released. My broadhead took him right in his transition zone.

Rolling terrain and a flat-shooting muzzleloader allowed Tim to kill this thick 8-pointer.

When It All Comes Together

The ground I hunt in Ohio is classic big woods with many of the features mentioned in this chapter. Here is an example of how the terrain affects deer movement.

In a favorite spot, there is a deep draw created by a mountain ridge with two connecting but opposing ridge spurs (Diagram A). A seasonal creek splits the bottom of the draw, about 250 yards at its widest point. Its banks are steep. On the upper end of the main ridge is a field of corn and whitetail clover. Adjacent to the draw and on the opposite side of the creek are several flat areas or benches that parallel the draw and connect to a couple of saddles and another smaller draw created by the two perpendicular ridges that meet on that side (Diagram B).

A strong funneling effect exists on both sides of the draw, and therein lies the question. Which side to set up on? The better question may be when to set up, because both sides are productive, with different move-

Deer Movements

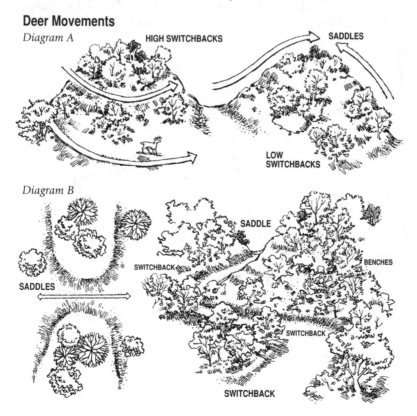

Diagram A   HIGH SWITCHBACKS   SADDLES

LOW SWITCHBACKS

Diagram B

SADDLE

BENCHES

SWITCHBACK

SADDLES

SWITCHBACK

SWITCHBACK

ment patterns. One side acts as a funnel connecting a primary food source to several bedding areas. The other side acts as a hub for several features that connect multiple travel corridors used by bucks to get from one bedding area to another.

Recently, I showed a friend, Chad Stearns, this find. An accomplished whitetail hunter, it did not take him long to realize that he was in the right spot. Chad scored the first day, tagging a 130-class P&Y buck. The night before, he had gotten the tour of the area he would be hunting and saw three good bucks in the corn and clover field. Hunting the field side of the draw in the morning was the ticket.

A few weeks later I was hunting that same stand. I placed a Tink's Smoking Stick on the upwind side of the trail coming off the fields and leading to the bedding area. I saw deer and by 10 a.m., I realized the rut was picking up. In fact, it was exploding.

High on my perch in the Baby Grand, I saw three different mature bucks running the benches across the creek on the opposite side of the big draw. I looked up at my cameraman, Chris Randall, and rhetorically asked, "You know where we're going to be tomorrow?" The response was, "Climbers?" I nodded.

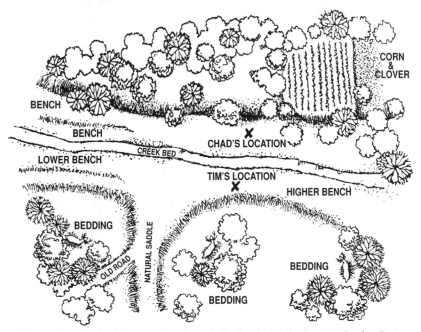

Tim made a sketch of the site where he and Chad took their bucks. Note his familiarity with the topographic elements, which give him clues to travel routes and bedding areas.

The next morning was a nightmare. A cold front was approaching from the northwest. The previous two days had been unseasonably warm, with most movement observed in the early mornings due to the big draw's ability to hold cool night air.

During the hunting season, the only thing I watch on television is the weather channel. If you are going to be serious about a commitment to take only mature deer, understanding frontal movement is important. A cold front pushes warm, moist air down as it moves through. To a hunter, this means rain and unstable winds followed by passage of the front, which brings cooler temperatures and steadier winds, usually from the north by northwest. (Write that down!)

Discover and use the topographic advantages, and you will put yourself in position to kill bucks that will make you extremely proud of making your commitment.

Sneaking up the creek, we could get to the benches without leaving much scent, but the hike up the steep hillside while short, brought on a good sweat. I hoped that a shower, the Scent-Lok suit and the Odor-Lock would do the trick. With two guys, it is always twice the chance of getting busted.

An early start, plus the overcast, gave us more time to choose the right trees for setting up. At daylight, rain began falling and the wind picked up. We were situated two-thirds of the way up the hill on a bench that was fed by a saddle and three draws.

The first buck came up the draw from the bedding area. He was nervous and far too small, with a broken tine. He turned right up the hill behind Chris' stand and went over the saddle, never knowing we were there.

An hour later, the rain was sometimes heavy, sometimes light. The winds were gusting and my confidence, and that of my camera operator, was waning. However, Chris understood that it was the rut and a buck could materialize anytime. Besides, we both wanted to get a television show "in the can" and that would not happen unless a good buck appeared.

The dreary day was suddenly interrupted by a distinct BUUURP! My eyes picked up the movement of a sapling above and to my right. A mature buck with high tines and a large spread was kicking the crap out of a tree. Chris was already burning tape.

The buck was headed up the draw, so I pulled out my open-barrel deer call and grunted. Nothing. I made a louder call with more authority. That got his attention. The buck started in our direction and then I spotted a doe! I adjusted the call's o-ring and let out a few excited fawn bleats. Simultaneously, it started to pour, and a gust of wind just about blew us out of our stands. Both deer disappeared and with them went the hope of a great television show and some fine venison.

Chris and I were soaked already, so we decided that we might as well stay out the rest of the morning. After all, the camera was still dry and in good shape. A rain cover and Chris' poncho had saved the day.

Another small buck, a 100-class 8-point, worked up the draw along the side of the creek from where we had come in. He meandered around below and behind our stands, and we checked on him periodically. After a while, he became alert and stared toward where the big buck had disappeared following the doe. The little buck turned and walked back the way he had come. The reason why was walking stiff-legged right toward us.

This was a good buck, really wide. The underbrush was sparse in the middle of the bench, and he moved comfortably through it; but as he neared the end where it opened into the hardwoods, there might as well have been a glass wall. He stopped and stared. The silence was broken by the twang of

If your neighbors are amenable and your property has any significant size, developing a quality deer management program will pay off within a few years. During the fourth year of management at River Ridge in southern Ohio, Michigan's Chad Stearns (left, with bow) took this trophy 4x4 and, less than a week later, Tim took a heavy-bodied 3x5 buck with a beautiful, wide-curving rack. The two bucks were taken in the same immediate complex of ridges and draws.

my bowstring and the telling whack of my arrow as it passed through the shoulder and both lungs on its way into the forest floor 40 yards below. The buck exploded off the bench, across the creek and halfway up the opposite draw, falling not far from where Chad Stearns had arrowed his buck.

Was there anything lucky about this morning? Maybe to hunters who rely on luck, but not to those who know about the topographic advantage.

Chapter 9

Get It In Gear – Camo And Clothing

When you know exactly what results you want to achieve, any job is supposed to be easier. Perhaps understanding your goal simply narrows the work ahead by focusing your mind. Maybe this is the secret. Once you make a commitment to reach out and seize something precise, you can cut a straighter path to it through the jungle of opinion, marketing claims and printed misinformation than if you were just going with the flow. That *hakuna matata* stuff is for the weekend warrior and that no longer defines you.

Tim's Louisiana buck. Of course, head-to-toe camouflage is the only way to hunt when you are in the field.

This chapter begins your odyssey through the gear you are going to need to begin taking big, mature deer every year. I am going to assume that during this time, while you are selecting and tuning up and practicing with your equipment, you will also be scouting hard, following the five precepts we laid out in the previous two chapters:

- Expanding your horizons

- Developing a specific written plan

- Understanding what deer are eating and why

- Putting boots on the ground with purpose

- Carefully selecting the information that will help you

In reality, trophy deer are taken with every kind of hunting set-up: long-bows with cedar arrows, crossbows, compound bows and, of course, firearms (rifles, shotguns, handguns and blackpowder guns). You can kill trophy deer with spears or with a rock. All you have to do is put the point of your spear in the buck's heart or through its lungs, and the rock just has to deliver the right amount of force to the most vulnerable spot in the deer's brain or spinal cord.

For the purposes of our commitment, however, I am going to limit what I talk about to the currently most popular weapons of choice for hunters and those with which I primarily hunt . There is a forest of conflicting opinion and direction out there, and we are going to cut to the heart of equipment selection, set-up and tuning.

If you want to consistently kill trophy deer, you are going to have to go to the field with good equipment ... or maybe you can do it with lousy gear as long as it works properly at the moment of truth. But frankly, deer hunting is hard and hunting for only mature, trophy deer is one helluva task. I said you could do it if you made a serious personal commitment, but I never said it was going to be easy. Good equipment, perhaps the best you can afford, will help eliminate the many ways Murphy can screw up your hunt. Therefore, if you are serious, you want excellent gear; you want to learn to take care of it and to maximize its performance. But first things first.

If you have made a commitment to take only mature deer, one of the first things I suggest you do is make an inventory. Take your hunting gear out of storage one Saturday and take a good long look at it. Does everything work? Do you need to float your rifle barrel? Does your bow scream like a pinched baby when you draw? Make a to-do list to refurbish your gear. Then, during the next few weeks or months, plow your way through it. Let's start with your camouflage.

Camo And Clothing

You do occasionally see hunters in the field dressed in Levis, an old shirt and a Detroit Tigers baseball cap. You can bet, however, that they have not made a commitment to taking only mature deer. These are either superbly careless guys who

- will soon become sick and tired of not seeing anything more than a doe or some fawns and will give up hunting with a bow in a year or two, or

- they are primarily outside for a nice stroll in the woods, or

- in a world of infinite possibilities, maybe they are such damn good hunters that they don't have to pay attention to what they wear or the direction the wind is blowing or whether their arrows are spined to their draw length and draw weight. Somewhere, there are probably individuals like that, but I do not know of any.

There are several good reasons why you should not dress in old, casual gear if you are a serious hunter. Old clothes are fine for just getting dirty and even for fishing. However, they were not originally designed to blend into the outdoor environment. They were designed to make you look good or to be functional in another environment. Old work pants retain odors from the days you adjusted the truck's timing belt or filled the lawnmower with gas, countless breakfasts of bacon and eggs, dog odors and even the softeners and brighteners in the soap from your wash. These are not clothes for success.

You need a minimum of two sets of camo and preferably three if you are truly committed to taking only mature deer. At a minimum, they should be made from a quiet material, and if possible, be both wind and weather resistant. I also highly recommend an additional set of camo more suited for cold and severe conditions. Throughout the hunting season, two sets of clothes should be rotated for primary use and a third set held back in reserve for Murphy. All should be kept in their own scent-free bag or container. I prefer the bags from either Tink's, Scent-Lok or Gander Mountain.

I have more camo than business suits. If you are serious about taking big deer, you are going to need camo that corresponds roughly to the season and the vegetation. In the early part of the season, I wear greens and browns – darker, denser colors – in lightweight material so I can hunt when it is hot. As the weather cools, the environment changes, and camo clothes with more contrast – perhaps a mixture of lighter and darker colors in the brown/black spectrum, with larger "open" spaces and bare limbs – are more appropriate.

Your objective is to select and learn to use hunting tools that will help you harvest deer like this every year. Remember that the equipment itself is not the objective. (Left to right, Ryan Klesko, Tim and Henry Rockey)

The look and feel of the higher grade of clothing than what I find in the local BoxMart suits me best, but in the early part of the season, in August and September, there is absolutely nothing wrong with stuff right off the *el cheapo* rack. As the season progresses in the northern states – and I have a Wisconsin friend who swears that the coldest day of his life was a damp winter day in a hunting camp in Alabama – you need more specialized clothing to hunt in comfort, and for this quality gear, it is definitely better to spend a little more. If you buy cheap for adverse weather conditions, you are going to be miserable, and a hunter who is not comfortable is a hunter who is not operating at his peak. It is hard to be alert for deer sign when you are shivering uncontrollably or pouring hot coffee from your thermos while wearing your mittens.

Does it matter what kind of camo you buy? And by that, I mean, what brand or what pattern? I have found that the heavily advertised camo patterns – primarily Realtree, Advantage and Mossy Oak – work just fine unless I am hunting in an extreme environment. There are so many specialized patterns that it is easy to find one to outfit a javelina hunt in Arizona, for example. Out there, you are really going to stand out wearing a dense green, woodland pattern. (In this case, even the old clothes might be better!) That distant sound of laughter is a pack of javelina rolling on the ground and pounding their sides.

Something about buying cheap gear is irritating, though. Buying camo that I know is only going to last one year before its colors fade or it begins to disintegrate makes me feel cheap, as if I am not giving my hunting ambition (my own commitment) the attention it deserves. When I was a kid, I wore coveralls and leather work boots when out hunting and still succeeded in taking does and button bucks, but that was normally all I saw – except at the check station. So, it's certainly your decision.

Ask yourself whether the clothes you are wearing help put you closer to your goal. In other words, do they bolster or inhibit your confidence, because in the chase for trophy bucks, your confidence is occasionally going to need some bolstering.

Whatever camo you decide on, keep it separate from your other clothes. Wash your camo separately in cold water with a non-scented soap that you can buy from manufacturers such as Tink's or Scent-lok. Then, dry your clothes on low heat or even hang them outside to dry. If you wash your camo clothes in hot water and dry them on a hot setting, you will cause them to fade more rapidly, and there is not much that is worse to the eye – and we believe to the eye of a deer, too – than bleached-out camo. Fading is simply a process of leeching out the dyes, and after that happens, you are left with dull whitish-gray material. White is fine if you are hunting musk ox or the winter season in Minnesota. For whitetails, white is a loser except in the heart of a snowy winter. Even then, it needs a pattern of tree trunks and branches to prevent it from being a solid blob, which might only be fine if you are lying down.

I probably should wash my camo stuff by hand, but I admit that I am too lazy to do this and use the family Kenmore. One thing I do recommend, though, is to run a cycle of hot water through the machine before you toss in your hunting stuff. This extra step will not take but a few minutes, and it removes a lot of soap and bleach residue left over from the last load of family wash. You can't be too careful.

If your camo has faded and is turning gray, get rid of it. Don't be tempted to even wear it around the house to rake leaves or paint the bedroom. Burn it. Cut it up. As long as it is hanging somewhere in the closet, you will be tempted to wear it. One Saturday, the alarm is going to wake you at 3:30 a.m. and – "Damn! I forgot to take care of my camo. I was so tired when I got home last week, and in the rain the electricity went out for a couple hours and … " See, if it can happen, it will. Even if you have to go to the BoxMart and buy the cheapest stuff they have, or if you have to wear black dress pants and a dark shirt, that outfit will be better than faded camo.

Some hunters hang their camo outside in the fresh air. I think that is an excellent idea. Of course, we unfortunately have to realize that our collective greed – pardon the politics – has poisoned the air and water faster than we can clean it up, so the term "fresh air" is somewhat old fashioned. Nevertheless, if we assume that the air quality near your home is similar to the air quality where you hunt, it should even out.

You probably do not just wash and dry your camo and hang it up in the closet, or do you? If so, you need to find a quality scent-free container for your hunting wear. Some people believe in placing things like scent wafers or a dollop of deer pee in their chosen container to help cover human odor, but I don't recommend it. The whole premise is to eliminate odors not create them. When it comes to you, no odor is better than any odor. A whitetail will be alerted to any foreign odor within its immediate area of detection. In reality, that means any odor molecule within the air in parts per billion either around the animal or carried by draft or currents. With that being said, I don't believe there's any harm in placing aromatic foliage or barks in along with your gear, such as cedar, pine or oak, as long as it is something indigenous to your specific hunting area. This only applies to non-carbon containers, as adding anything but your hunting clothes would defeat their purpose.

After bagging up your clothes, find somewhere to hang the bag, so it will be far away from perfume, after-shave odors, gasoline fumes and/or dog and cat hairs.

Not an easy task these busy, crowded days, but if you work at it, the right place to store your aroma-sensitive gear should materialize.

Do not forget your boots and hats. Ever since the popular television show *Magnum PI*, in which Tom Selleck wore a Detroit Tigers baseball cap to chase bad guys, a lot of people from spit-on-the-floor outdoorsmen to get-down young rap stars have adopted an attitude about headgear. You are not a gumshoe or a kid in the 'hood. Be cool somewhere else. You have chosen a different path.

Because so much heat radiates from your head, you need to carefully choose the kind of hat you wear and how to take care of it. Treat your cap or hat like any other valuable part of your hunting gear. In warm months, a cap provides shade for your eyes; in cold months, it keeps your brain warm. A hat keeps dangerous ultraviolet waves off your sensitive skin, too. Those are valuable functions.

If you have never paid much attention to your headgear, start now. Pull on your hat and go outside to practice shooting for an hour, or just go for a walk. When you are done, take your hat off and feel the damp inner lining, and on hot days, feel your damp hair. Just like your underarms or your crotch, dampness and heat escaping from your head means that odors will be present there, too. So, take care of your headgear like you would any other

In his continuing conversation with Dr. Karl Miller, a well-know deer biologist, Tim discovers the scientific reasons why good camouflage and scent-blocking clothes are vitally important in your quest for mature animals.

Deer Vision and Hearing

Tim: Why do deer see so well? Do they have eyes in the back of their heads?

Dr. Miller: Well, several reasons. As a prey animal, a deer's eyes are mounted on the side of its head and the eyes protrude slightly from the skull. A deer can't see directly behind itself but it can see about 310 degrees, so it just seems like they have eyes on the back of their heads.

Two additional factors are the size of a deer's pupil and a reflective membrane on the inside curve of the eye. The large pupil lets in more light than a human's during low light conditions, about 10 times as much. And the reflective membrane allows light entering a deer's eye to pass over its rods and cones twice. This is why they can run through the woods at night and not crash into trees.

Tim: If they can see so well, how can they detect the least little movement but miss me completely sometimes when I should be clearly visible?

Dr. Miller: Light entering an eyeball is focused. Humans, who are ultra-sensitive to color and generally have very acute vision, have about 150,000 cones in this focus area. Deer have far fewer cones in proportion to the number of rods. We think this gives them greater sensitivity to movement than to color.

In addition, a deer's eyes seem to share a characteristic common among some grazing animals. They see a wide horizontal band rather than focusing on a spot. We think this enhances their ability to detect movement.

Tim: So you are saying that we hunters see better during the bright part of the day while deer see better at night and in low light conditions.

Dr. Miller: Exactly.

Tim: Okay. The million-dollar question: "Do deer see in color?"

Dr. Miller: Without getting too technical, deer apparently see some colors, but not all that we see. Their vision seems to be similar to that of a person who is color blind in the red-green spectrum. Blues, they see very well, but they can't distinguish clearly between reds and greens. So leave the blue jeans at home. And brighteners in detergents enhance the colors deer are sensitive to. Blaze orange should be in every hunter's wardrobe. We see orange well, but deer have a hard time distinguishing it from the other colors of the forest.

Tim: What about hearing? Why is it that every deer for half a mile hears me clear my throat or slide a boot on my treestand?

Dr. Miller: Good question, and the answer may surprise you. Based on research at the University of Georgia by Larry Marchinton, David Osborn and Arthur Stattelman and other studies done – by Kenneth Risenhoover at Texas A&M, for example – it doesn't seem that deer hear any better than we hear.

Compared to us, deer have unique ears, though. They are quite large and swivel independently. If a deer looks at you and swivels his ears in your direction, he's got you. So, if you see a lone deer, pay attention to its ears. If it frequently cups one or both ears to the rear, for instance, you can bet there is a deer following.

What we believe at this time is that because deer are 24/7 residents of the woods, they inherently understand every sound that is native to the woods. Therefore, the sound of your arrow scraping ever so silently across your arrow rest or the click of a safety sends it bounding away. It knows those are foreign noises and therefore – because it is a prey species – threatening.

An understanding of the mechanics of deer vision and the role of camouflage will help you select stand sites such as this one high in a fir tree.

item of essential camo. Keep your hats clean and odor free. Do not wear them to the grocery store or while you are throwing the football with the kids. If you cannot wash them, a sprinkling of baking soda on the inside will help reduce lingering odor.

Treat your hunting boots the same way. Unless it is extremely cold – in which case I wear special snow pack boots with rubber bottoms and heavy, replaceable felt liners – I recommend high-top rubber boots. It is hard to damage good rubber boots, but if you spill oil on them when you are monkeying around with the car, they will never be the same. Of course, you want to do everything you can to keep them clean and dry on the inside, too.

Activated Carbon Suits

Speaking of caring for your hunting gear, I believe in the beneficial properties of the new suits that use activated carbon to capture human odor. I wear one almost all the time when I hunt. Scent-Lok says that when human scent molecules are exposed to their fabric's carbon fill, the molecules are drawn in and attach to the millions of microscopic pores and crevices of the activated carbon.

Scent-Lok says this is called "adsorption," not absorption. We are familiar with the absorption of sponges or cotton camo when it rains, because we soon get damp and then we get cold. It's hard to hunt like that. I have heard that the hardest mental and physical part of US Navy SEAL exercises is when trainees are continuously cold and wet. From my experience, I believe it. Activated carbon apparently attracts odors like a magnet attracts iron filings except that iron filings cling to the outer surface of the magnet rather than saturating the material like your scent does with the carbon fragments. Imagine the molecules of your human odor clinging to the carbon in the suit rather than evaporating with sweat into the air and gently wafting downwind to the nose of the neighborhood's dominant buck.

Another property of these suits, manufacturers claim, is that they allow the relatively free passage of air, thus wicking moisture out, away from your skin. I have hunted in a lot of damp polypropylene and cotton outfits that are supposed to have these same wicking properties, but after a little while, I have mostly just felt wet and irritated. Based on my experience, the manufacturers of activated carbon suits have gotten it right.

The problem with a carbon suit on a long trip is that every couple of days you need to find a laundromat. Not that the suit gets dirty in the conventional sense, but according to Scent-Lok, their suits will adsorb human odor for about 40 hours. After that time, the carbon becomes saturated and needs to be cleaned. Fortunately, you can do this easily enough by running the suit through a couple cycles in a hot clothes dryer. The temperature inside needs to reach 150 degrees and remain at that level for 30 to 40 minutes to restore the carbon's ability to adsorb odors again. Actually, you read conflicting figures on this, but you certainly must run commercial machines on their hottest setting.

I have read at least one account of a writer spraying the inside of the dryer with a scent neutralizing spray before putting his carbon suit inside. While I do not have hard evidence one way or the other, I am suspicious of

A Scent-Lok activated carbon suit is wonderful for "adsorbing" human odors. The straps and buckles over the suit are the full-body harness Tim uses whenever he climbs.

the ability of a light spray to remove the carrying oils and scents of commercial fabric softeners. Leaving the dryer door open for a while helps it air out as does running it empty on hot for a few minutes and cleaning out the lint build-up in the dryer vent.

If your carbon suit gets dirty as in truly muddy and snotty, it is usually okay to toss it in a standard washing machine. Again, I recommend that you run a hot-water-only cycle first, because this will help remove soap and fabric conditioner left over from earlier washings. Then use a detergent marketed to hunters and wash the carbon suit in cold water. After a complete washing on gentle cycle, rinse it again in cold water. There is no need to reactivate the carbon only to go to your stand smelling like a box of Arm & Hammer soap.

You need to take care of a carbon suit a little differently than your other hunting garments. As soon as you take a suit out of the dryer, put it in a carbon-lined bag or some other heavy plastic bag. Carbon-lined storage bags are available from the suit's manufacturer. One of the vacuum-sealing gadgets – essentially a heavy plastic bag and a little pump that sucks air out of the bag – that is currently being advertised on television would be perfect. Scent-Lot says not to put any scent wafers or other type of scent in the bag with the carbon suit because the idea is to be totally scent free.

In the field, put your suit on only when you are ready to walk to your stand. Do not wear it while driving with a cup of coffee in your hand or gassing up the truck or anyplace else where the suit can pick up foreign odors. Then, as soon as you get back to camp or to your truck or even a little earlier if possible, take the suit off and get it into the plastic bag. Do not wait until after you have eaten to remove it or its activated carbon will adsorb the odor of frying bacon and the hot sauce you are liberally sprinkling on your scrambled eggs.

This brings up the use of another hunting tool, an odor-eliminating spray. I spray boots and clothes even when I wear an activated carbon suit. I also wipe down my bow and quiver and even spray a rag and wipe down my guns, backpacks and climbing treestands. Anything my hands touch that can carry odor into the field, I swipe down with an odor neutralizer.

Some authorities say that deer can smell us more than a quarter mile away through dense woods. That is far enough to ruin most hunting set-ups. While I don't believe that we can totally eliminate body odor – I mean, it is a natural function, a by-product of being alive – we can dramatically reduce the amount that we let fly downwind. Which brings up another small subject – and I am only going to touch on it briefly, I promise – that, according to women I have hunted with, is particular to the male persuasion: scratching, burping, farting and spitting. When it comes to particularly egregious bodily functions, the golden rule is to do the right thing.

These fine deer were killed with muzzleloaders by hunters who exploited the "topographic advantage" philosophy outlined in the previous chapter to narrow the range of travel-route possibilities.

I freely admit that I indulge in one unpardonable offense. Every now and then – and every day when I am not flying – a pinch of tobacco finds its way into my mouth. Friends tell me to my face that it is a disgusting habit and maybe it is, but if they truly do not like it, they can find some other friends, who are cleaner, better people than me.

Nevertheless, I recognize that they have a point. The smell of the processed tobacco juice I spit is definitely not a natural smell in a buck's habitat unless I am hunting down south in tobacco country. Some counties in North Carolina and Virginia overwhelm deer with tobacco odor, but even then, it is not the same. So this is about all I can say in my defense. Chewing tobacco may not be welcome in every person's parlor, but when I am outside hunting, fishing or changing the oil in the truck, I am probably going to have a chew. I don't recommend it, and I say this recognizing that the tobacco smell may on more than one occasion have spooked a big deer. I am sorry. It is my right to choose how I want to screw up. I think it may actually help a little, especially during the rut, when I'm on stand maintaining vigil from dawn till dusk. This is my special weakness, but I sure do love it; and I am not going to stop, so I will just have to work harder. If you chew or smoke, you do not have to apologize, but understand that you will have to work harder.

Chapter 10

Get It In Gear – Your Archery Equipment

What brand or style of bow you choose is not especially important. Whether you shoot with a longbow, compound or a crossbow does not matter either. All three are effective. The only thing that matters is whether you accurately place your arrow in the vitals, and the only measure of effectiveness is whether you can hit your target in a hunting situation.

A commitment to take only mature big-game animals will set you apart from average weekend warriors. First, there will be a price, but if you are dedicated to your goal, the payoff will be enormous.

Most bowhunters shoot a compound bow. It is what I'm primarily familiar with and what we are going to discuss, the compound and the accessories that help you maximize its buck-killing potential.

People frequently ask what kind of bow is best. Of course, that is an impossible question to answer. It is like asking what kind of car is best. I shoot a Mathews because it suits me. It fits. It is rugged, fast and dependable. It is technologically advanced, and I have the utmost confidence in its ability to perform up to and even beyond my expectations. Plus, I can make it shoot almost whisper quiet.

Still, I know that most other companies build excellent shooting equipment too: PSE, Bear, Hoyt, Martin, Bow Tech. I am not saying that all companies are equal. I am saying that company names rise and fall in popularity. In the '50s, Pearson was king, but today, the name has virtually disappeared. In the '60s, it was Jennings, and in the '70s, it was Bear. These brands are barely hanging on. Maybe in the '80s, it was PSE and in the '90s, certainly Mathews. Certainly both of these companies are still strong. I personally do not believe it matters what brand you choose, so pick one, get to know it and stick with it like I have done with Mathews.

What matters more than the name of the bow company are things like quality and reliability. What matters is how much confidence you have in it. What matters is how well you shoot it. I recall a friend on a bear hunt in Ontario a few years ago who said that when a bear finally appeared at his bait station, it looked enormous. It had to be the boss bear of the woods. That bear was so big my friend lost confidence that his 55-pound compound bow and three-blade broadhead could take it down. He took a deep breath and made a perfect shot, however, on a bear that squared about 6 feet and whose skull measured practically 20 inches. His confidence wavered, but he used his gear effectively.

Making a serious commitment also means that in order to be successful, you must consider bowhunting, because in most areas of the country, the archery season begins before the rut and runs through the peak of the rut. In many states, particularly in the South, the archery deer season continues into the following year. These days, most states have legislated the gun seasons to slivers, sometimes less than a full week. Therefore, if you can learn to drive a sharp piece of steel through the heart of one of the world's wariest wild animals, a big mature buck at that, you are indeed Da Man!

All kidding aside, you have simply got to be an all-season hunter! A-hook-in-the-water-every-day-of-the-season kind of person! I call it maximum intensity mixed with extreme patience.

Cost

Does a $700 bow shoot better than a $400 bow?

Remember that commitment thing we talked about a couple chapters ago? You will not be honoring it if you waste your money or your time working a second job to pay for the most expensive bow in the retailer's shop, the one with the prettiest stickers and the hottest bells and whistles. On the other hand, who was the fellow who said, "Crap in, crap out"? My advice is to do the best you can with what you can afford, and I'll leave it at that. You can honor your commitment and make your dedication to taking only mature deer pay off if you buy good equipment, with "good" being defined by reliability, consistent performance and local support.

Use every gear advantage, Tim says. Technology and human inventiveness are the two things that separate us from our 24/7 quarry.

Speed

Every archer talks bow speed, but, of course, they mean arrow speed. If you don't take any other tip away from this section, take this one: you do not need a bow that shoots 300 feet per second (fps). In fact, I do not imagine that half the bows you see advertised as capable of launching an arrow 300 fps could possibly be tuned by the average guy to shoot that fast, stay together for more than a hunting season and launch repeatable arrows. Once you get to that speed or any speed above about 260 fps, your bow is going to become difficult to handle. Anything and everything can go wrong. The draw-force curve shows you a short, hard draw to maximum weight and then, if you fudge forward even a quarter inch, the cam (or cams) will try to roll over and that bow is going to jerk your arm right out of its socket.

I enjoy the fellows at the range and on the pro-shop shooting lanes who are real speed freaks. They are having fun, and I get a kick out of listening to how they tweak their bows to perfection ... and work more hours to keep them tuned. I pick up some ideas. They twist the string and play with the buss cables; they install speed buttons; they do away with the traditional metal nock stops and use serving as a stop instead; they experiment with different types of string and number of string strands. This is all excellent stuff, but let's face it, these archers enjoy the technical challenge of archery. They are usually the first to try new sights or interesting new broadhead designs; and they are the first to broadcast their opinions about them, too. If you have a technical problem and the pro-shop bow mechanic cannot be reached or gives you advice you do not trust, these guys will often be able to help you.

Nevertheless, your focus is on taking mature deer, not having a fast bow. I'm going to bet that most of the techies and speed demons at the shooting lanes never put a really big mature deer in their sights, and if they did ... well, there is my bias against people who talk a good game versus those who are quietly but effectively taking care of business.

I am a commercial jet pilot by trade, and I enjoy speed as much as anyone; but I know that regardless of the speed of your bow, it is your hunting and shooting ability that makes the difference between whether you kill a big deer or not. You want to spend more time hunting, scouting and practicing and less time tinkering with your equipment. These days, you can definitely get lost in the morass of "bow tuning," and after you have spent endless hours fiddling, tinkering and measuring, you will not shoot any better than before you started.

"Bow tuning" has become an industry in archery, and it is my view that this has ultimately been harmful. It's as if bowhunting has been taken over by the science nerds in the class. Pick up any archery magazine for the last 5 years and there will be articles on what you have to do to make your bow shoot better, complex things that not only involve your bow, but your arrows and accessories, too. Why are manufacturers selling us gear that is not ready to go hunting and to perform at its peak when you buy the stuff? What's their problem?

You are not going to shoot perfectly. World-class 3-D champions like Randy Ulmer and Alan Conner do not shoot perfectly. World-class bow-hunters like Chuck Adams do not shoot perfectly. Olympic gold-medal archers like Justin Huish do not shoot perfectly. With his particular snap-shooting style, I am sure that Fred Bear missed more than he ever let on.

If you are committed to taking mature bucks every year, you are probably not going to win your club's 20-yard indoor winter leagues. If you cannot make or train yourself to shoot perfectly, are you going to feel guilty about it? Are you going to lose confidence in your ability to hit what you are shooting at? The "bow-tuning" debate is nothing more than "complexi-fication" that makes a mountain out of a molehill, and I personally know archers who beat their brains out checking, changing and worrying about every thing on and about their bow. To be endlessly concerned about bow

A few basic tools are essentially all you need to keep your bow in hunting shape: set your nock, adjust your draw weight and check alignments. For the very highest quality tuning and most precise arrow flight, you will need to spend hours fiddling, checking and tweaking your gear's alignment. Intense tuning efforts are required to win 3-D tournaments, but hunting requires that you consistently hit an 8-inch pie plate at 30 yards.

tuning is going to ruin your enjoyment of archery, and when that happens, you are finished as a bowhunter.

The second problem with the endless bow-tuning debate is that it keeps people out of our sport. Call it what you will – sport, hobby, avocation, passion – but if hitting an 8-inch pie plate at 20 yards looks too terribly complicated, and if the people who are already doing it do not seem to be having fun, folks are not going to want to participate.

Now, to many bowhunters, this sounds great. They wish everyone else would quit and leave the deer and elk, the shining, dew-spangled mornings and the solitude of the forest to them. Get real, friends. That is never going to happen. We lose 10 to 15 percent of archers every year, mostly because they give up on ever taking a deer with a bow. If we do not keep bringing our kids in and educating the public, our numbers are going to diminish to insignificance in the point of view of political impact and wildlife management. Two and a half million bowhunters is not a lot of archery voices in a modern America of 300 million people.

So, to end this matter, let me suggest that, if it is possible, you go to a pro shop when you look for a new bow. Explain to the owner or the salesman that you want a solid, forgiving, reliable bow that has a good reputation and a great warranty. You do not want a low-end bow or some radical reflex contraption. Make sure the shop will continue carrying that bow line, as shops often change brand loyalty. You must be able to get your bow serviced locally. You do not want to send it to the factory to be re-cabled, for instance. That will take a month, regardless of what the company advertises about customer service. Get the pro shop to show you a number of hunting bows that meet your specifications for draw length and draw weight. Then, shoot them. If you cannot shoot them, do not buy there unless you do not have any other choice.

Two or three tips will be useful when you are selecting a bow. First, do not overbuy. If you are smart enough to have a budget, be smart enough to stay within it.

What if you cannot afford a high-end wonder bow? Why not find, through the pro shop, the people who bought last year's hottest models and now want to trade up? Why not make them an offer for their used top model? When you get to be rich and famous by taking the Super Slam of North American big game and have a dozen great big whitetails to your credit, go ahead and splurge on the most expensive bow in the shop. Know in advance, however, that such a bow will not help you attain your goals any faster than the one you are using now. And, if you really do accomplish the Super Slam and get any publicity at all, manufacturers will line up to give you free stuff. The secret is that shooting ability, putting the broadhead into the deer's vitals, comes more from an inner source of discipline and self-control than from the equipment you are hauling into the field.

There is a tendency to measure a little too long for draw length. Chances are you are going to be shooting with a mechanical release and, if you are serious about hitting what you are aiming at, a peep sight. This means you do not have to draw the bowstring consistently to the corner of your mouth or have it touch the tip of your nose as you draw and aim. Your anchor can float. You probably do not want it to float from one side of your head to the other, but even if it does and your dominant eye acquires your target in the center of your peep, well so what?

The danger is that you will have a bow with an adjustable draw length and when you try it on the pro shop's shooting range, you will draw it with your fingers and not have your release with you. Women tend to shop and study their purchases, but men buy stuff in a hurry and often on impulse. Impulse is bad when you are buying a bow. So, if you drove to the pro shop and forgot your release aid, turn around, go home and get it. You cannot be measured properly if you shoot with fingers at the shop and with a release when you hunt. The mechanics, as well as the dimensions, are different.

Selecting And Matching Accessories

Shoot with a mechanical release, not with fingers. Top-level competitive archers and bowhunters whom I respect all agree that when you change from shooting with your fingers via a tab or a glove to shooting with a release, you tighten your groups by 25 percent. It is not scientific, but it is a consensus figure. Out to 30 yards, that can mean the difference of a foot or so, and that difference is a hit or a miss or possibly the thin line between a quick kill and an ugly wounding shot.

Most bowhunters shoot with releases today because a release makes them more accurate. No, releases are not as traditional as shooting with your fingers wrapped around the string. (Okay, Ishi did not shoot with a

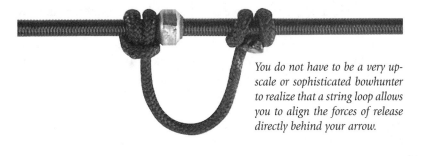

You do not have to be a very up-scale or sophisticated bowhunter to realize that a string loop allows you to align the forces of release directly behind your arrow.

mechanical release, but he died almost 100 years ago. If he were alive today, he would use one.) Some people even question whether a release violates the basic definition of a bow as a hand-held, hand-drawn, hand-released instrument. They wonder whether using a mechanical release moves you toward firearms or – horrors – a crossbow.

If you let this murky philosophical thinking sway you away from using a release, fulfilling your vow to take only mature deer is going to be harder. Your effort is to find ways that are legal and ethical, within the spirit of the hunt as well as the letter of the law, to make fulfilling your commitment easier. A release makes your job easier. Use one.

Archers first used peep sights on recurve strings. With the increased energy and dramatically increased arrow speeds that today's hot bows deliver, a peep is necessary for precision shooting. A peep fits into your bowstring above the nock. It can be round or oblong or even square. When you draw, you pull the string to the valley, and if you have everything set up right, the hole in the peep centers in front of your eye. In the exact center of your peep, you will center the proper distance pin or the correct pin gap.

Most archers serve their peep, which means they tie it on the string to make sure it will not move, before putting a drop or two of Super Glue over the ends to lock it in place. When you shoot a release, your peep serves as a rear anchor and helps you pick a spot. When shooting with fingers in the old

Tim shoots with a peep sight on his bowstring and a mechanical release in his right hand.

days, anchor point was extremely important, but today, with fast compounds and releases, we talk about a "floating anchor point," or the fact that a lot of bowhunters don't come to a precise rear spot each time they draw.

A peep helps you solve left-right shot placement problems that are the result of a floating anchor because it requires you to focus through the center of the hole. These days, peep alignment is often the most accurate part of an anchor.

Most archers use a smaller aperture peep for competition, about 1/16-inch in diameter, and a larger aperture for hunting, about 1/4-inch in diameter, because you never can tell what the weather will be like. You are most frequently going to take your mature deer when the day is at its dimmest – in the early morning or late evening – so I want a larger hole when I use a peep for bowhunting.

Numerous aperture sizes are available, and several manufacturers even make peeps with removable apertures so you can change the size of the hole as the light changes. That is a great idea when you can sit quietly at a table and carefully pull one of these very small apertures out of the peep, store it in a baggie and find the larger or smaller one that you need. Unfortunately, accomplishing that on a treestand while you are wearing gloves is going to be difficult. Find a peep with a fixed-aperture size that is good for low light conditions and use it exclusively.

When the leaves are down, you need to climb higher so that you will not be so easily observed by deer at ground level.

A comfortable seat for your treestand, such as the AirRide from Gorilla, will allow you to hunt for longer periods without squirming and standing.

One potential difficulty using a peep for hunting is that it will not align when you draw. Release shooters have an easier time with this than finger shooters who typically twist the string and, therefore, must be more conscious of peep alignment. When you draw the string with a release and everything is set up properly, the peep comes back to your eye perfectly every time.

Another potential difficulty using a peep is string stretch. Synthetic strings may be stronger than steel, but when they warm up or are continually stressed, they elongate. When this happens, your settings can change. It is always a good idea to draw and check peep alignment with your sights before you climb into your treestand.

Peep sights have pros and cons. You will hear a lot of archers curse them. They say that as it gets darker they cannot see through their aperture. Apparently these bowhunters haven't practiced very much because they would know what their light limits were before the moment a buck walked within range. More refined detractors claim that they use a peep with a wider aperture to avoid any low light problem, but it is so wide it does not help them center their pins. Nevertheless, for ultimate accuracy when you are shooting with a release, use a peep sight.

What about sights? Almost all bowhunters who shoot compound bows use them. Famous Oklahoma archer Jim Dougherty has had a hugely successful bowhunting career using a compound bow without sights. Jim began bowhunting with a recurve 45 years ago, and he does a number of things differently than most 21st-century bowhunters, including shooting with fingers instead of a release. This great bowhunter is certainly one of a vanishing breed.

In a sense, it does not matter what kind of sight you use as long as it helps you hit what you are aiming at. For most bowhunters, the standard four- or five-pin adjustable sight is going to be the first, best choice. These sights can be moderately expensive, but there is no reason that an inexpensive sight cannot give you quality performance. Here is what to look for when you go shopping:

- Look for a sight that is rugged and all metal. I have an aversion to anything plastic sticking out on the front of my bow and that includes plastic pin guards. I have been suckered by too many manufacturers of products from automobiles to kitchen appliances that substitute cheap molded plastic parts for the real thing, metal. Plastic does not belong in a hunting camp or on a treestand.

- Look for a sight with pins that lock down tight but are easy to adjust. You cannot afford to book a hunt at a lodge far from home only to spend your first day re-setting your sight pins. You want a sight that will survive bouncing on the rack of a four-wheeler. Whenever I travel, my sight pins always seem to need tweaking, though, and this is a good reason to carry a hex-wrench set in your daypack.

• Look for a sight with pins that are both thin and bright. Fiber-optic pins are terrific, as were the old Saunders T-Dot plastic pins from a generation earlier. Do not worry, though, if your sight does not have 10 feet of fiber-optic cable wrapped around the pin guard. Although that effect looks cool, there is only so much light information a strand of glass or plastic can emit, so the shorter ones should be fine. Fiber-optic strands come in various diam-

This wide-racked buck was not as thick in the beam as Tim originally thought, but it was the result of a difficult shot that caused him to lean backward and shoot around the tree that held his stand.

eters. I recommend the thinner rather than the thicker diameter (a personal preference), but when a manufacturer mounts a pin in its bracket, he melts the tip facing you so that you have a flatter and wider surface area than just the end of the clipped fiber optic strand.

• Look for a hunting sight, not a target-style sight adapted for hunting. Round pin guards have come into fashion lately and you hear that because the hole in the peep is generally round, a round pin guard will help your eye focus better. Round is fine, but so is rectangular or hexagonal. If you have a super deer walk into your kill zone, and your eye does anything other than put the correct pin on the vitals and then focus on the spot, there is something wrong with your attention span, not your equipment. For hunting, I find that the more delicate adaptations of competition sights – they invariably come with round apertures, levels, up-pins and so on – are not sufficiently durable or versatile in the field.

• Look for a pin sight that mounts by a dovetail bracket. When you travel, even if it is only to your neighborhood food plot instead of a cross-country road trip for Columbian blacktails, take the sight off the riser and store all your gear inside a cushioned hard-sided bow case. It's also not a bad idea to find a small soft case to place it in. Remember to etch the sight bar at the exact ends of the mounting bracket so that you can re-mount the sight precisely.

I don't use, nor do I recommend using, a pendulum site. My biggest difficulty with them is that where they might work well from 5-30 yards, they have moving parts and those parts have the ability to make noise. So, check this before you buy one and make sure it is not more aggravating than the inherent angular correction it gives you.

Let's return for a moment to the 5-to-30-yard range of most pendulums, because I feel that it presents a fundamental problem for a committed bowhunter. If you are proficient with your equipment and you are serious about taking mature deer every year, you are going to want to shoot beyond 30 yards. Now, I want to be the first person to urge you to shoot only within your effective range. If you are only accurate or only have confidence out to 20 yards, for heaven's sake, don't take the 30-yard shot.

On the other hand, many self-appointed archery gurus would like everyone who shoots a bow and arrow to confine themselves to 20-yard shots, but that is rubbish. The modern compound bow and its accessories are designed to let you shoot perfectly at two and even three times that distance. Olympic archers shoot accurately out to 100 yards with a lightweight recurve! Sure, many factors, including the wind and weather, have to be taken into consideration before you take a long shot. Is the target standing still and does it present a broadside or quartering-away shot? Are you certain of the distance or are you just guessing? Have you consistently practiced shooting that far?

No one who takes mature whitetails every year limits themselves to 20-yard shots. It is an interesting idea that has been foisted on us by the puritanical in our crowd, but it is not practical in real life. The truth is that you must limit your shooting to whatever distance you are confident that you can make a quick, clean kill, and that distance varies by circumstances and by individual. Therefore, pendulum sights are fine if you are hunting in dense thickets where you cannot see beyond 30 yards, but otherwise, nothing has yet been invented that can replace the versatility of a standard metal, dovetail pin sight for best-all-around-bowhunting service.

This brings us to the important subject of your arrow rest. Perhaps I ought to wait for the next chapter where we discuss arrow tuning, as the rest and the arrow must initially be conceived as a single mechanical unit. The arrow rest is the ultimate guide for your arrow. If you think of the string as a propulsion mechanism, the rest is the only part of the bow that provides arrow guidance. So, the arrow rest is very important.

Rattling antlers fall into the fun and learn categories of hunting accessories.

There are several styles of arrow rest. Finger shooters use a "shoot-around" rest because the string leaving the fingertips slides out and around them. This sideways motion during the forward thrust of the string loads kinetic energy in a multi-directional fashion into the column of the arrow shaft. In other words, the force vectors are not straight or in-line. So, your arrow shaft flexes or fishtails from side to side as it moves forward, which may cause it to strike the bow riser. This is a big source of inaccuracy. In the old days, a spring-loaded, Teflon-tipped Berger button screwed into the arrow rest's mounting hole in the riser took up some of the sideways pressure and prevented the arrow (unless your release was really awful) from clacking against the riser. The Berger button also held the rest in place or, if a stick-on rest was used, projected through it.

Small things are important. A rope to draw your gear up to your stand, for instance. Tim believes that the most effective stands will be out of a deer's normal band of vision.

As I have said, relatively few bowhunters release the string with fingers today, and most shoot modern compound bows. So it is safe to say that the majority of arrow rests purchased at a pro shop or mass merchant are "shoot-through" rests. This means that the rest is set up to work in combination with a release. A shoot-through rest supposes that the forces propelling the arrow will be almost 100 percent straight. Launcher or speed fin support for the arrow is, therefore, not in the older shoot-around 3 o'clock and 7 o'clock positions, but rotated around to the 4-5 o'clock and 7-8 o'clock positions. The arrow is balanced equally on two support armatures and the cock feather on a three-fletch arrow passes cleanly between the two fins. A separate holding device keeps the arrow in place on the rest.

Recently, the old idea of a drop-away arrow rest has been resurrected, and the marketplace has been flooded with them. Many drop-away rests work well, and a few do not work at all. The idea behind a drop-away rest is to provide support at the critical instant of take-off and then to move the support device out of the way so they cannot interfere with the fletching. Fletching/rest interference will cause you to shoot very inconsistently. I like the idea of a drop-away rest, but adding more moving parts, things that can fail at the wrong time (Is there a right time?), scares me … better choose wisely.

If you go this route, I highly recommend Trophy Hunter's "Shaky Hunter" or the "Drop Zone" made by Trophy Ridge.

These two styles of bow holders will allow you to either hang your bow next to your seat or to stand it in a bracket attached to the platform.

My suggestion is to buy a solid, simple shoot-through or drop-away rest, one without a lot of brass and color-coded tuning and adjusting gizmos, and then practice enough with it to make sure you understand how it works. Find a secure way to keep your arrow on your rest, too, as there is nothing more heartbreaking than doing all the work to get in position to take a big, mature deer only to have the arrow fall off the rest while you are lifting the bow into position. Goodbye season.

A great deal has been written lately about stabilizing and silencing your shooting. Not too many years ago, if someone used a wrist strap and tied or served a pair of rubber-strand Cat Whiskers on their bowstring, they believed they had sufficiently addressed this issue. The wrist strap has two functions. It allows you to shoot with a relaxed grip, and it gives you the confidence that after a shot you will not drop your bow. All of this is a way to keep from gripping the bow riser tightly, thereby twisting (or torquing) it and affecting the left-right placement of your arrow. With a wrist strap, a properly stabilized and lightly held bow can rebound or rock forward away from the archer after a shot, and it will not swing back to hit you in the face.

A wrist strap allows you to shoot with a relaxed grip, and it gives you the confidence that you will not drop your bow after taking a shot.

Tim has occasionally taken smaller bucks for his television show North American Fish and Game. *Here he poses with Dale Palmer (back) and Bob Robb.*

Cat Whiskers and String Muffs quieted the noise of a shot because they broke up the harmonic pattern of the string's oscillation after release. Energy was released explosively from the vibrating string as noise. Of course, we now know that the amount of noise produced by a good hunting recurve 25 years ago was exceptionally small compared to that from a good hunting compound bow today.

Manufacturers are spending a lot of time working on the noise and vibration problem in state-of-the-art bows. A good pro shop will carry a dozen different devices, which can help your hunting in three practical ways:

- They keep the bow steady in your hand.

- They reduce the after-shot vibration that eventually causes accessories to work lose, limb bolts to back out and limbs to fail.

- They help limit damage to the joints of your elbow and shoulder if you shoot a lot. This is also a problem for traditional shooters who shoot high poundage bows.

Spend some time browsing and checking out all of the possibilities for your bow. You want to carry a lightweight set-up, but a heavier bow absorbs more "shot shock" than a lightweight bow. This means that ounce-for-ounce, with a heavier bow you won't feel so much "slap" in your hand when you shoot.

As a general rule, except for speed buttons, anything attached to your string and limbs is going to slow down your arrow. Nevertheless, I like to silence my shooting. I favor a hydraulic hunting stabilizer, string silencers and other similar damping accessories. My Mathews is equipped with innovative harmonic and string damping, which in itself is more than sufficient to fulfill my demands. When it comes to a choice between arrow speed and a forgiving bow shooting controlled arrows, I'll take the slower combination any day. At the distances we generally shoot, we learn trajectory by continuous practice, and even with a 275- to 300-fps arrow, a buck can "jump the string" at 30 yards.

Chapter 11

Get It In Gear – Broadheads And Arrows

To a hunter, a great bow and the finest accessories in the world are useless without a perfectly straight arrow tipped with a razor-sharp broadhead. This combination drives home your message, so there is a little tweaking to do before you head for your treestand.

The whole point of matching your gear is to put technology on your side.

Your Broadhead

Most bowhunters are opinionated about their broadheads. I am. I like a head that cuts immediately, as soon as the leading edge touches a buck's skin, and I can get downright argumentative about my preferences.

In my experience, archers will argue about broadheads until they are exhausted from the sheer stupidity of other points of view. In fact, they are more obstinate about their broadhead of choice than about their bows. It is a good thing there are almost as many styles of broadhead as there are bowhunters, which ensures that there is much to choose from and argue about.

The truth is that most commercial broadheads work just fine, although I have serious reservations about many of the mechanicals. Replaceable-blade heads are the standard today and they can be tuned to fly true, cut easily and penetrate rapidly. Whatever head you choose, make sure you select one that will not lose its blades if it hits bone.

The number of blades in a broadhead, their thickness, whether they are vented and what style of tip they have is less important than how well they fly with your arrow. A large or heavy head requires that you increase the size of your fletching because the arrow needs to rotate in flight to stabilize quickly.

Now this is a broadhead! The Game Tracker First Cut EXP Magnum 125. I think this cut-on-contact head is ideal for hunting big whitetails or, for that matter, any big-game animal on the North American continent.

Stable, accurate broadhead flight is essential to penetration. For recurves and longbows, the rule is the heavier the head the better the penetration. Searching for greater arrow speed, compound shooters have moved in the opposite direction, to smaller, lighter heads with low-profile blades. These lighter heads and shorter, lighter arrows have helped boost arrow speeds well above 300 fps – about 200 mph – but penetration is an issue with light, fast arrows and heads. By itself, speed does very little to promote arrow flight or accuracy.

Properly mounting a broadhead on an arrow shaft means the tip of the arrow will be in line with the center of the arrow shaft. Then when you release, your bowstring moves forward and pushes the arrow straight ahead. You want that thrust to load the column of the arrow or deliver the bow's stored energy to your shaft without angled force vectors to torque the arrow in any direction except toward the heart of a big buck.

A properly mounted head that is in line with the centerline of your arrow spins in a more or less fluid manner. A head that is not in line will wobble perceptibly.

Another test for arrow flight is natural: take your broadhead-tipped arrows outside and shoot, perhaps into a foam target, after you have established a group using field points. Shooting broadheads into the hay bales that are customary on public practice ranges is dangerous.

Blades that must move to open when a head meets its target define a class of broadheads collectively referred to as expandable, mechanical or, most commonly, open-on-impact. Theoretically, with all makes and models, these heads fly like a practice point, penetrate like a fixed-blade head and cut like a sharp replaceable-blade head. It is a wonderful idea. Archery engineers have worked on the concept for a generation at least, studying concepts like "rotational momentum" and "gyroscopic stabilization" that mean little to most of us.

Regardless of their engineering and design, mechanical broadheads remain a controversial topic in archery. If the fundamental concepts actually work, the benefits to hunters (and perhaps in a curious way to game animals as well) are extraordinary. Still, the practical difficulties are large, and the ultimate benefits are arguable. In my experience, you should exercise extreme caution with expandable broadheads.

The latest innovation in broadheads is called "hybrids," where a cut-on-impact blade is accompanied by two expandable blades. My experience with these has been nothing but phenomenal! This great marriage of aerodynamic principle and penetration results in a devastating combination, and I highly recommend their use for taking whitetails and other big game.

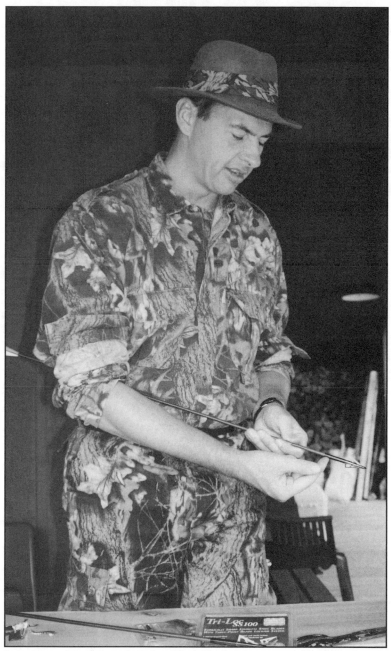

It is not your bow that needs tuning, Tim believes; it is your arrow and arrow launching system. After all, this is your ultimate point of personal introduction to a deer.

Let's Talk Arrows

We archers need a fundamental understanding of kinetic energy (kinetic energy = 1/2 x mass x velocity^2) because it is a measure of the penetrating ability of our arrows. Good penetration with a broadhead-tipped arrow means plenty of slicing and bleeding. This results in quick, clean kills. Dead deer in 60 seconds or less with a clean shot through the vitals is a big step toward your commitment to yourself.

You want enough energy in your arrow to achieve total penetration, a complete pass-through. Do not even listen to any other argument. When pre-historic hunters shot game, their flint arrowheads certainly remained inside the animal. Because their spears and arrows did not pack enough energy to punch completely through and kill an animal like a deer quickly, we believe those hunters often used poison-tipped arrows. You cannot tip your arrows with poison, and besides, bow-and-arrow dynamics are different today. The idea that a broadhead should remain inside an animal and continue to cut and chew up its insides as it runs is discredited by experience and testing.

Your only penetration standard should be an arrow tipped with a balanced, super-sharp broadhead that passes cleanly, quickly and completely through a deer. This gives you an entry hole and an exit hole, both leaking blood. Because most deer are shot from treestands at close range, it is important to have a lower exit hole for a blood trail.

The larger the game animal, the greater the energy you need for a quick kill. For 100- to 200-pound deer, 50 foot-pounds is sufficient; less is acceptable with precise arrow placement. For larger, heavier animals like elk or caribou, you should step up your arrow's energy output. (A foot-pound is the energy required to raise 1 pound of weight 1 foot against gravity.) On the face of it, kinetic energy is simple. The formula for calculating kinetic energy in foot-pounds is speed (in fps) squared and multiplied by total arrow weight in grains (including your broadhead). Then, divide by 450,240. Under laboratory conditions, an arrow with 50 foot-pounds of energy should theoretically penetrate twice as far as an arrow with only 25.

Studying the formula, many bowhunters figure that a fast, light arrow should give them greater kinetic energy. That is only partly right because a light arrow absorbs less energy than a heavy arrow. Consider a 500-grain aluminum shaft and 100-grain broadhead that fly at 250 fps. If you switch to a 400-grain carbon shaft with a 75-grain head, you will pick up about 10 fps. HOWEVER, the heavier arrow delivers 83.3 foot-pounds while the lighter, faster arrow gives you 71.3 foot-pounds. The lighter, faster arrow has about 14 percent less energy than the heavier arrow! At 20 yards, this may not be a huge difference, but as distance increases, the lighter arrows loses energy faster than the heavier arrow. The 600-grain arrow still has more energy at 40 yards than the 475-grain arrow. This may mean 6 or 7 additional inches of penetration!

Shooting heavier arrows is one way to improve penetration. Another way to increase arrow energy is to increase your draw weight. Crank your bow 5 more pounds, and you will pick up an arrow-energy increase of about 10 percent – and gain speed with a flatter trajectory, too.

Remember that straight-flying arrows out-penetrate wobbly arrows. For deepest penetration, you want your arrow's energy directed down the centerline of the shaft. When a flexing arrow hits game, the shaft whips to the side. This reduces the energy available to drive your shaft through a deer. A true-flying arrow puts all its energy behind the broadhead. To achieve this end, you have to spend a few minutes on the arrow charts and consider arrow spine and shaft size.

Arrow Spine

We grade or measure arrow shafts by their spine or stiffness. Understanding spine helps you match the right arrow to your bow. This means they hold it on both ends, hang a weight in the middle and measure how much it bends. (For more on this and other technical topics, please refer to the recently published *Archer's Digest* by Rick Sapp from Krause Publications.)

Spine indicates how much your arrow bends when it leaves the bowstring. It has to fly several yards before it recovers its straightness. All arrows flex. Your job is to minimize that flexing so your arrow achieves rapid stability. If bending occurs at the right frequency, the arrow will fly true; otherwise, the arrow flies poorly. When you use a mechanical release, your arrows flex up and down. Strings released with fingers cause the arrow to flex side to side. Correctly spined for your bow set-up and physical characteristics, a shaft will flex little and recover fast.

For best arrow flight, you must buy the proper arrow shaft. The same arrow flies differently from your 45-pound carp-shooting recurve than it does from your 70-pound, 75-percent-let-off, single-cam deer hunter.

Once you release the string, you still control the bow and its attached accessories, but the arrow and the broadhead are gone. You cannot take it back, so it is critical to find the arrow and broadhead combination that flies best for your set-up. To help you, arrow manufacturers offer an array of arrow sizes and instructions. Each manufacturer has a selection chart matching shaft sizes with your arrow's length and point weight, your draw length and draw weight, and the type of bow or cam: wheels, hard twin cam, one cam, recurve, etc. If your arrows are not shooting well, consult an arrow chart to make sure you have the right shafts.

Weight and Balance

Lightweight carbon arrows fly faster and with a flatter trajectory than aluminum arrows. That is the good news, but that is not all the news.

No arrow absorbs all of a bow's potential energy, and light arrows absorb less than heavy arrows. Some heavy arrows absorb as much as 80 percent of a bow's energy. This means light arrows leave more energy behind in the form of vibration, shock and noise; and you feel a shot much more in your hand, your bow set-up needs to be checked more often to be sure things do not rattle apart, and your shot is noisier. The noise of a fast shot has to be dampened and a variety of accessories are available to do that.

Because they absorb less energy, lighter shafts do not penetrate as well as heavier shafts and this can complicate your selection of broadheads. You are aiming at flesh and bone, so complete pass-through penetration is crucial to a good blood trail.

Light, high-speed arrows are more temperamental than heavier, slower and more stable arrows. Unless you execute a shot perfectly, light arrows are likely to fly poorly.

An old rule of thumb recommended 9 grains of arrow weight for every pound of draw weight. For a 70-pound bow, that would mean shooting a 630-grain arrow! This formula is old, but the principle of using draw weight to determine arrow weight still applies. The absolute minimum for a hunting arrow with broadhead should not be less than 450 grains, give or take a few grains.

Take a minute and think of your arrow as if it were an airplane and not a projectile. Both have to meet a few of the same basic requirements in order to defy the laws of gravity and sustain balanced flight in order to get from point A to point B. Let's focus on the effect balance has on whether an airplane or, for the purposes of this discussion, an arrow will fly well, poorly or not at all. Both have a nose and a tail, and in between, a body. Here's the real deal. Neither will fly if one end is grossly heavier than the other, and both benefit from the additional aerodynamic stability of wing surface. Both objects have a center of gravity, and depending on length and weight, this has a profound effect on how well our object flies through the air. On an aircraft, this is referred to as a percentage of mean aerodynamic chord as related to the center of gravity (CG), and on an arrow it is referred to as the FOC ("Forward of Center"), which is also related to the CG. Therefore, if you really want to get your broadhead-tipped arrows to fly at optimum capability, you'll need to pay attention to the FOC. You'll first want to take your hunting arrow and measure the length from tip to tip. Mark the center or the halfway point. Then take the arrow and balance it on a narrow flat surface. Your hunting knife will work nicely (don't cut yourself!). Record the distance between the center and the balance point. Taking this figure, dividing by the full length and multiplying by 100 will give you the FOC. You're looking for 9-11 percent. Optimum balanced flight for broadheads will be between 10-11 percent.

Should You Choose Aluminum or Carbon?

Until recently, every bowhunter shot aluminum arrows. While aluminum is still popular, carbon has become the dominant shaft. Aluminum shafts are amazingly consistent in size and weight, straight to tolerances as fine as .0015 inch. They are inexpensive and repairable, although in my experience, a straightened arrow will never fly perfectly again. Aluminum arrows will do the job.

Terry Rohm took this fine buck when hunting with Tim in Texas.

Carbon is characterized by smaller diameter and lighter weight shafts. Even at their maximum length and stiffness, carbon shafts are lighter than aluminum or wood. This characteristic allows a speed advantage for the archer who wants a fast arrow but wants to keep kinetic energy high.

Penetration tests using foam targets give carbon shafts the edge over comparably spined aluminum, due mostly to carbon's ability to retain more energy and, therefore, deliver more on impact. Physics cannot be denied! Aluminum arrows are created by pouring molten metal over a mold to form the shaft. Carbon arrows are a combination of fibers layered to form the shaft. This in turn makes for differentiating the two in how they absorb and retain energy and also how well they affect stabilized flight and downrange performance. This is a mouthful, but simply stated, the slow motion photography/video shows that the aluminum arrow never stops flexing in its attempt to direct the energy. This is sometimes referred to as the "wet noodle effect." The carbon arrow, on the other hand, will quickly stabilize directional energy and not flex again until impact, which results in having more stored energy to deliver than the aluminum arrow. The bottom line is that today's carbon shafts will give you more performance, and as a committed hunter, you'll want every advantage. Early carbon arrows were extremely expensive, but the developments of new grades of carbon and carbon-composites and new manufacturing methods have made carbon shafts competitive with aluminum.

Attention to Detail: Fletching

Fletching gives your arrow stability in flight. You want arrows to begin rotation, like a rifle bullet fired from a barrel with twisting internal grooves, as soon as it clears the bow riser.

Ever since man began shooting the bow and arrow, feathers have been used to stabilize arrows. They are not as popular today because of competition from plastic vanes. Perhaps 90 percent of all bowhunters and competitors use vanes for arrow fletching, and I disagree with this preference.

Plastic has a reputation for durability. It does not become wet and heavy, either. Feathers are lighter, and although they flutter like plastic and are a little noisier, they are arguably a couple feet per second faster. For every reason to choose plastic, there are equal reasons to choose feathers.

I prefer big, 5-inch helical cut feathers to stabilize my Carbon Express CX 400 arrows. Shooting a 32-inch carbon arrow from my 75-pound bow, I need big feathers to help guide the broadhead-tipped arrow after it leaves the string.

Attention to detail is important – a large, cutting broadhead and 5-inch feather fletching for arrow stability make things possible for Tim.

Velocity tests conducted by independent archery engineer Norb Mullaney suggest that a feather-fletched arrow will still be traveling 4 fps faster than plastic 29 yards downrange. Therefore, at normal hunting ranges, feathered arrows travel faster, drop less and arrive sooner than arrows with vanes.

Trueflight argues that feathers coming in contact with the bow or arrow rest produce less interference than vanes. Feathers fold down out of the way and then pop back up. Plastic vanes, because they are more rigid, bounce the rear of the arrow out of alignment. This deflection causes substantial arrow "swing," which is aggravated by a plastic vane's weight and lack of "grip." The superior guidance that feathers provide also helps prevent yawing and fishtailing, the oscillations that increase drag and slow an arrow down.

Bowhunters who hunt from high stands need to shoot completely through deer for a quick kill and an easy blood trail.

Feathers give more stabilizing guidance than vanes, and they give it faster. The surface of a feather has a slight roughness that causes a rippling disturbance in the airflow over it. Trueflight calls this "grip," a concept that has been tested successfully on racing-yacht hulls competing for the America's Cup. When an arrow "yaws" or flexes to the side, this added grip helps realign it faster than a smooth plastic vane.

When the base of your arrow swings to the side, aerodynamic forces are pushing it away from where you aimed it. Due to the sluggish straightening ability of plastic vanes, the arrow oscillates from one yawed condition to another. This gradually decreases, but feathers decrease it faster than vanes. Yawing costs speed, range and accuracy. What's more, penetration of a yawed arrow is lower than an arrow flying straight because the yawing action dissipates energy sideways as the arrow's head attempts straight-line penetration.

The weight savings with feathers also helps stability. Weight added to the rear of the arrow makes it less stable. Add too much weight on its rear, and the arrow will try to swap ends!

A feather's ability to fold down when it hits something eliminates any large initial swing following contact. The lighter weight of feathers adds to the stability of the arrow, and the "grip" adds further to straight flight. These advantages mean that consistent arrow flight is more readily achievable for arrows fletched with feathers. An arrow with feathers tolerates a wide range of bow variables and some errors in shooting form, too. Finally, with feathers, your arrow rest is less critical and requires less time to set up.

Feathers are more tolerant of variations in shaft spine, bow weight and a poor release. In field conditions, not every variable is controllable. Slight variations in shooting form are normal. Time, terrain, obstacles and cross-winds are all potential sources of error. The feather-fletched arrow simply deals with these variations best.

The knock on feathers is that they are noisy and soak up moisture. A rain-soaked feather will change your shooting because the weight is greater, and a wet feather does not respond as fast as a dry feather.

Noise is an area where fletching with vanes is superior to feathers. Roger Grundman of Flex-Fletch says that when it is quiet, you can hear the flight of a feathered shaft. So today, when we archers are doing everything we can to silence our shooting, this is an issue because vanes have very little game-alarming flutter.

Hunters interested in the latest gear and high arrow speeds typically switch to vanes, but high performance set-ups involve more energy, higher forces and lower flight times, so stability and solid guidance are even more important. Vanes tend to magnify errors of form or imperfections in equipment.

Plastic's flexibility and stiffness can change with changes in temperature. In cold weather, plastic is stiffer and more rigid. In hot weather, plastic is more flexible, less rigid. This variable definitely affects arrow flight and bow tuning.

In Easton high-speed videos, plastic vanes "flap" or ripple when the arrow is shot. This oscillation begins immediately at release due to the low strength-to-weight ratio of plastic, and it continues as the arrow flies downrange. The same videos show that feathers react differently to launch, very quickly regaining an upright and stable posture even at speeds above 300 fps.

Climbing higher gives you some benefits, but it makes some demands as well. You can see more, but your shot angle becomes steeper and the kill zone narrows.

Plastic vanes cost less than feathers and are easier to mass-produce. Feathers are grown individually, of course, on white birds. They are plucked and cut by hand; the bases are ground and the feather is dyed. All of this is significant from a point-of-view of cost and time associated with hand labor.

Size Matters

Many bowhunters like a small vane to keep the arrow's weight and friction profile at a minimum. Whether they are plastic or feathers, larger vanes stabilize better than smaller vanes. Don't forget you're a hunter and will be shooting broadheads!

Generally, a 5-inch, 3-fletch or 4-inch, 4-fletch will give you good results on broadhead-tipped arrows. High-speed bows shooting wide, heavy broadheads may even require something in the 5 3/4-inch size.

Bowhunters shooting high-speed bows typically shoot a stiff arrow tipped with a lightweight, perhaps even a mechanical, head with little more profile than a field point, not a "wide, heavy" broadhead.

Archers debate whether the shape or orientation of the vane is important. In the end, it does not matter, but conventional wisdom suggests that to cause just the right drag or friction to help steady your flying arrow point, an offset (glued at a slight angle to the centerline of the shaft) or helical (curved slightly around the shaft) mount is important to help the shaft rotate in flight. Like the rifling in a gun barrel, this adds gyroscopic stabilizing. Helical and offset fletching produces more rotation and stability than straight-mounted vanes.

With fletching, the final word is that whatever size, style or orientation you choose, make your arrows uniform so that you can reliably tune for smooth, straight flight.

Chapter 12

Get It In Gear – Bows, Guns And Other Tools For Success

We should quickly review a few issues that are on every bowhunter's mind. If you are square about things like whether you want a fast or forgiving bow, you are going to go to the field with greater confidence in your abilities and your equipment.

Paul Meeks killed this superb whitetail west of the Mississippi. Tim's hunting theories will work wherever there are deer.

Your Bow's Let-Off

Compound bows with high let-off are four or five times more popular than bows with lower let-off. Years ago, bow let-off of 50 percent seemed high. These days, the average compound has a 75 percent let-off, and manufacturers offer optional modules for 65 percent and 85 percent, although many people would argue that a bow let-off that high makes a fast bow almost unmanageable.

The Mathews LX is an example of the trend to lower holding weights. At just 35 inches axle-to-axle with a 6 5/8-inch brace height, this bow is rated for IBO speed (5 grains of weight per pound of draw weight) at 317 fps with 65 percent modules and 315 fps at 80 percent let-off. At this speed, 2 feet-per-second is nothing compared to the advantage of an additional 15 percent let-off. The difference is between holding almost 25 pounds at the lower let-off and only 14 pounds at the higher let-off.

A bow with a low holding weight should be easier to aim and shoot effectively, allowing you to put your arrow right in the buck's vitals, but high let-off bows are finicky. They have steep draw-force curves, so if you allow the string to creep forward only slightly, the cam is going to try to roll over and let the arrow go. It is easy to let down with a 65 percent let-off bow. You can feel the cams rolling over and the bow will give a jerk, but the snap is manageable. If you decide to let down a high let-off bow, be prepared for an unpleasant moment wrestling with the string when you are sure your shoulders are going to snap together beneath your chin. Let down an 80 percent let-off bow on your treestand, and you could be jerked right off the platform.

String silencers are still very useful in quieting your shot and are easy to tie on your string. A super-fast, high-energy bow may tear them up quickly, however.

Tim was attracted to this deer's unusually tall headgear.

The issue with let-off involves the widely accepted (at this time) book-keeping organization devoted to bowhunting, the private Pope & Young Club (P&Y). P&Y's record book was originally designed to honor North American trophy game animals, not the hunters who kill them. P&Y's founders imitated the older Boone & Crockett Club's ideals, standards and measuring system. The difference was that minimum scores were lowered dramatically for game taken by bow. The most recent difference is that P&Y has taken political stands, ruling that electronics (sights, ranging devices, sight lights), crossbows and compounds with let-off higher than 65 percent make a big-game animal ineligible, although the 65 percent rule has recently been modified – grudgingly. The small group of senior members has also voted in secret to remove individuals and their game animals from the records for reasons other than equipment or game violations. If the senior and regular members do not like you personally, you will never advance in level or status within P&Y either, because vacancies within those very small ranks are filled by secret ballot, not by longevity.

Today, P&Y's elitist structure prevents it from moving forward with the times. You will have to make up your mind whether you wish to support the established system at this time, because it has no impact on your personal commitment to take only mature big game. It simply becomes a matter of whether you need to see your name listed in a very long column in very small print.

Fast and Forgiving

We bowhunters make a distinction between forgiving and unforgiving bows. A standard for forgiveness has been a bow with a 7-inch or greater brace height. The benefit of greater brace height is improved bow efficiency. A high-brace-height bow typically lets you shoot a lighter, thinner-walled arrow and that results in greater arrow speed. With the advances in bow design resulting from consumer demand for fast, quiet, short axle-to-axle bows, the traditional thinking about brace height may not be universally true.

The true improvement is actually not so much speed as it is a flatter trajectory. At 240 to 260 fps, which is a great speed for consistent, no-problem shooting, you can misjudge yardage to a 40-yard deer by a yard or so and still place your broadhead in its vitals. At 300 fps, you can misjudge by twice as much and still collect your trophy.

On the down side, faster means greater tuning problems and a bow that is less efficient, less forgiving. Any "wasted" energy not transmitted to the arrow becomes noise, vibration and a sore elbow on your bow arm.

A slower bow launching heavier arrows or with increased draw weight is more efficient. Slower is quieter, too. Slower arrow speed not only means less time tuning, it means that there is less stray energy left over in the system after the arrow escapes.

Most pro shop owners believe that a 240 to 260 fps arrow speed is as much as the average archer can successfully tune for and shoot consistently, even with feathers. Beyond that speed, the stress on your bow becomes so high that unusual things can happen, things the average guy can't predict or prepare for: handle flexing, cam lean and so on. The typical paradigms react in a chaotic manner and hence the switch by hunters to mechanical heads which fly like darts. (How they hit and penetrate is often another story.)

Speaking of cam lean, I believe that all cams lean when bows come from the factory, and this should be one of the things you immediately correct. You can fix this by adjusting your cable guard and twisting the bowstring.

What About Firearms?

Hey, I believe in chucking rocks if it's legal and they'll sell me a license! Hunting with firearms is solely dictated by state, province and season, and how that season coincides with what the deer are doing at that particular time in the region you'll be hunting. In the topographic advantage, we previously discussed how hunting methods are affected by pressure, movement patterns and other variables. Here, we'll cover the basics of what I think is important to meet the demands of the hunting conditions, not dictating what is the perfect firearm. As I said before, that will be determined by the agency controlling the hunt. The rest is strictly preference.

My whole philosophy on whatever you choose to hunt with is that you better be damn proficient with it! The biggest mistake I have seen, and it is like a disease, is that a huge percentage of those hunters who hunt with firearms spend minimal time, other than a few days prior to the actual hunting season, prepping and practicing with their guns! That firearm should be like an extension of your body. If you're tracking big mature whitetails in the expansive woods in northern Maine, like my friends Shane and Lanny Benoit, then you need to be just like them and able to snap a Remington 270 pump-action carbine up to your shoulder and hit a 6-8 inch pie plate at 80 yards every time – even if it were tacked onto the side of a moving piece of plywood!

Granted, most people are amazed at the Benoit's ability to consistently locate, track and kill mature whitetails every season, but I wasn't surprised at all. I knew it from the first minute of having met these two distinguished hunters. I could tell by what they knew about whitetails, their commitment to taking only mature deer and the intensity that exuded from their shared stories – hey, my kind of people! What's not so apparent to most hunters are how critical their choice of firearm is and also the degree of marksmanship that is connected to their unending success, as it pertains to their particular style of hunting.

So, how do you go about choosing the right gun or guns? The first step should be to decide what style of hunting best describes your preferred method of hunting. Determining whether you will be stand hunting, still-hunting, tracking, driving/pushing or spotting and stalking will go a long way in determining what firearm you choose.

Another method for determining your firearm of choice is to gauge the requirement for the killing shot. Under what conditions will it be taken? Will the deer be feeding, running, bedded or alert and ready to bolt? Will you be hunting in dense thickets, open hardwoods, in a field, in the desert or in extreme conditions? And finally, how will your hunting location determine the range at which the shot will most likely be taken?

Each one of these variables presents its own unique set of requirements that needs to be considered if you wish to hold true to your commitment of taking mature deer on a consistent basis! Whether you're hunting with a rifle, shotgun or muzzleloader, there will be choices to make concerning action, sights, optics and performance, as it applies to ballistics and ammunition. There is certainly no lack of options in today's world of firearms!

In addition, knowing what type of firearm is legal in the area(s) you plan to hunt will help you narrow your search for the right firearm or

Table 2: Boone & Crockett Club Random Survey of Firearms Used to Take Trophy Bucks (1993)

Caliber	Total Responding
Shotgun Slug	509
30-06	283
270	128
30-30	122
7 mm magnum	73
308	72
Muzzleloader/Blackpowder	28
Shotgun shot (loose)	13
	1,228

firearms. In fact, this factor may make the decision for you, since certain areas only allow certain types of firearms to be used. This, obviously, wasn't always the case. In the past, our forefathers had old "hot lips," the Pennsylvania long rifle that hung above the open hearth and provided the venison one day, while repelling the "lobsterbacks" as they pressed Chad's Ford near Brandywine creek in July 1777 the next. There was one gun for many jobs. You, on the other hand, will have to decide if you'll be hunting Delaware County (muzzleloader only), Bradford (shotguns only) or Sullivan County (where rifles are allowed). And this only gets more complicated as you hunt outside your home state. Bottom line here is to be sure to check those regulations!

Accuracy

Before heading into the timber, it should be apparent by now that your commitment will not be complete until you are proficient with your chosen firearm. Time on the practice range will pay off handsomely when the first shot opportunity at a mature buck is the only one that will be needed to end your hunt on a good note. Just as in bow hunting, practice should be as realistic as is allowed. Assuming that you followed through on choosing the right firearm to match both your style and anticipated conditions, the correct method is to practice like you hunt and hunt like you practice. This is a bit of an over-used cliché, but it is the mindset you'll need to instinctively make better and more accurate shots when you really need to. You will get much more out of this approach. Besides accuracy, your knowledge of ballistics and ammunition, as they apply to your required shooting style, will improve the performance of your firearm.

Also, engaging a professional gunsmith to assist you in customizing your firearm will also make you a better, more accurate, marksman. Some common adjustments to make hunting firearms more accurate include trigger modifications, floating your gun barrel, customized scope mounts and sites, and matching the stock to your shooting style.

Firearms In-Depth

There is an expansive amount of reference material available on specific types of firearms. It is full of in-depth information on rifles, shotguns and muzzleloaders. Once you've chosen your type of firearm, obtaining more information will help you maximize your proficiency on the practice range and in the field. Authors that have written books on firearms that I highly recommend include Bryce Towsley, Dave Henderson and Tom Fegley.

Handy Tools To Make Your Life Easier

Global positioning systems are now the standard in knowing where you were and how to get there again! With the help of satellite triangulation, outdoorsmen can literally find their way around the world in the dark or in zero visibility. Nothing is better at helping you find the stealthiest route to and from your treestand in the dark, avoiding detection from that big buck you've been hunting.

If you cannot find topographic maps at your local sporting goods store, you can find waterproof topo maps for sale online at maptech.com, thanks to a combined effort by Maptech and MyTopo. Just log on and select your area. The advantage of using MyTopo maps is that you can enter your chosen area and possibly eliminate the need for multiple maps of regions that lie along the edge of a standard USGS topo grid. Plus, the cost is only about $15 per map.

You may never need an outdoor survival tool, but hundreds of hunters, hikers, campers, boaters, bird watchers, photographers and fishermen die each year because they could not get help when they needed it. Get a compass and a whistle. These items are cheap and effective. Carry them with you, even when you are absolutely certain you know the lay of the land and perhaps especially then, because pain can quickly cause a fog of disorientation, even when you are hunting in your backyard.

A whistle should be your number one survival item, and it should be in your front pocket where you can reach it easily if you become injured, not in your backpack or even in your fanny pack. The piercing scream of a whistle can be heard many times as far as a human scream. When you run out of breath from screaming or run out of energy after you have fallen or gotten lost, you will still be able to blow that whistle.

The compass is your second essential survival item. You will probably never use it if you are hunting locally, but it just may be needed that one time when you slip …

Have you ever blundered around in the dark looking for your treestand? Of course you have. Everything looks different when it is dark. Every hunter has gone astray on mornings so dark and with a flashlight so dim that you couldn't see the orange surveyor's tape that marks the path to your stand. The familiar trail disappears. Distance judging becomes impossible. How do you think this affects deer, especially big mature deer? Not well, I can assure you. Because you are professionalizing your approach to hunting, you have to get over this sloppy behavior. Buy an item such as Fire Tacks, trail markers that glow when you shine your flashlight on them, in sufficient quantity that you can find your way in the dark. Get to your stand early and get ready. Expect to see a big deer. Floundering around in the woods is both self-defeating and a form of self-sabotage.

A rangefinder should be in every serious bowhunter's pocket, especially those who are committed to taking only big, mature whitetails. Rangefinders are not expensive, and they are invaluable when used to check your distance before a shot or when you are just practicing. It is instructive to guess distances and then either pace them off or verify them with a rangefinder. This helps solidify your yardage-estimating abilities and your confidence. You can practice anywhere, and the more diverse locations, the better you will become: in the neighborhood when you are walking the dog, when you are pheasant hunting, in the long hallways of a hospital or on city streets where there are many distractions. By and large, the more we practice, the more we realize that estimating distance accurately is difficult. Imagine then, how much more difficult it is when a trophy deer is strutting its stuff nearby, and you are fighting off "buck fever."

The difference between preparation and the real thing is that unless you are diligent and rehearse shooting from a treestand, your practice will be done on the ground while your actual shooting will be done from somewhere up in the tree canopy. If you are launching an arrow from 24 feet (8 yards) in the air, a 20-yard straight line distance from the base of your tree to a big buck means that you will be shooting at a down angle an actual distance of about 21-1/2 yards. Also, during firearms season, those rare long shots out beyond 100+ yards occasionally arise when hunting transitional areas like expansive fields between the timber.

The reasons to use a rangefinder outweigh the reasons to not use one. Yes, a rangefinder is one more "thing" to fumble around with on a treestand, and there is the almost certain fact that a buck is going to appear precisely when you are turned in the wrong direction. And yes, you probably need two hands to operate one successfully. Still, the fact that a rangefinder can give you a precise distance reading is reason enough to buy one, to practice with it and then trust it when the time comes to pull the trigger of your release or firearm.

There are two kinds of rangefinders: lasers and coincident mirror. Most laser rangefinders are shaped like binoculars. When you gaze through the eyepiece, a superimposed crosshair aids in aiming. Just press a button and read the LED distance display. Depending on the model, a number of options can be called on such as changing modes for different weather conditions or based on the subject's ability to reflect light.

Lasers operate by emitting a light pulse that strikes the object in your crosshairs and is reflected back to the unit's receiver at the speed of light. Since laser light travels in a straight line and at a constant speed, the time it takes the pulse to leave and return is calculated internally, and a distance in yards or meters is displayed.There is some distance measuring error in a laser rangefinder. The closer you are and the harder your target the better. Swarovski's laser guide with 8 x 30 objective lenses is +/- 1 yard out to 1000 yards. Of course, a laser rangefinder only works because something is reflecting the laser beam directly back into the objective lens of the unit. The fine print for these types of units notes that the laser is accurate depending upon the nature of the target. A reflective object like an automobile is accurate to 1200 yards. A hard solid object like a tree trunk is accurate out to 1000 yards. A soft solid object such as a deer is accurate to 900 yards, and a moving object such as a running mule deer is accurate to 700 yards.

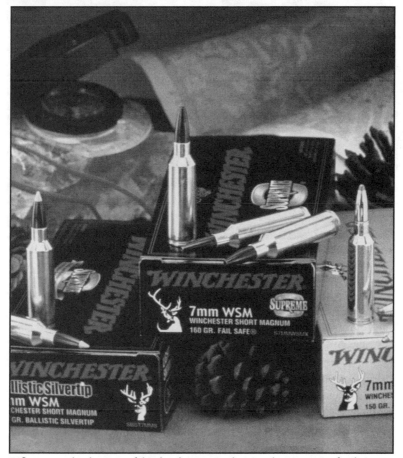

Riflemen need to be as careful as bowhunters in choosing the accessories for their gun. Several sizes of high-quality ammunition are usually made to fit any modern gun, and they must be carefully sighted before you go into the field.

Having the right equipment makes your rcommitment to hunting only mature deer much easier.

Pocket-sized coincident mirror rangefinders do not need batteries, and they can easily be readjusted if you drop them. "Coincident" means that dual mirrors give you a split image through the viewfinder. When you align the images with a finger-operated focus wheel, the distance is read on the internal scale. Distance can be determined in any weather, and the ranging function is not affected by hand tremor. With a 98-percent accuracy level and a price tag much less than that of a battery-powered laser rangefinder, these are great values. Its minimum range is 10 yards and maximum range is 75 yards with an advertised accuracy of +/- 1 yard at 50 yards.

Chapter 13

Tips, Tactics And Some Friendly Reminders About The Basics

Scent Control

Whitetails do not carry day planners. They rely instead on keen natural senses and instinctive behavior to guide their movements from day to day. Their instinct is the immediate growl of one of their stomachs and the arc of the sun and stars. Except during the rut, their behavior is entirely defensive.

Tim uses Wind Floaters (his invention) to verify wind direction on stand.

The primary defense deer possess is not a keen ability to reason their way out of a threatening situation but rather their sense of smell and an instinct to react immediately and sometimes violently. Some scientists estimate that a whitetail can smell ten thousand times better than a human! After all, a deer has several hundred million scent receptor sites in its nose compared to, for example, a mere five million in an average human nose. So, to be successful year after year, I know that a hunter of trophy whitetailed deer must take every possible precaution to control the odors from his body and his gear. Give them no reason to run and hide!

For several generations, we have tried to fool a whitetail's incredibly talented nose by using a variety of artificial scents and lures. Fifty years ago, because the smell of a striped skunk was the strongest and most awful in nature, outdoorsmen used bottled, imitation skunk scent – carefully – to try to disguise their own odors. In the '60s and '70s, millions of gallons of product designed to confuse or overpower the deer's nose with an odor other than that of the human body were packaged in tiny bottles and sold to hunters. For almost half a century, ownership of a popular "cover scent" was more lucrative than printing fake $50 bills.

Then, in the '80s, several inventive individuals adapted the odor-dispersing technology pioneered by pet supply manufacturers to the hunting conundrum. These scent-eliminating sprays and washes were designed to minimize the ability of odors to become airborne.

Although countless millions of dollars of scents, lures and odor enhancement and dispersal gadgets have been sold to outdoorsmen, most of it heavily hyped and advertised, there is not a shred of scientific evidence that any of it is very effective. There is only the anecdotal testimony from hunters about how well or poorly these products actually work. We know that stuff fools our noses, but we also know that humans are lightweights in the nose, beak and muzzle department.

About 12 years ago, field suits with built-in pouches of activated charcoal began appearing, and this kind of product has actually seemed amenable to giving hard evidence that it is effective at "adsorbing" odors. Adsorption (we also discuss this in the first gear chapter) is the ability to attract oily odor molecules and bind them lightly on the surface of some material like, in this case, charcoal. Absorption, like a sponge, is the ability to soak up internally, to become filled. Both processes, adsorption and absorption, allow the fundamental material to become clean or odor-free again. Activated charcoal becomes relatively clean when you place the garment in your home dryer and run it through a couple of cycles on the hottest setting. You can wring out an absorbent material like a cotton shirt and it can dry completely by evaporation. For it to give up an odor, however, you would have to soak the cotton shirt with a "wetting agent" like a detergent that dissolves the oily odor molecules before you washed it.

Thousands of hunters have tried suits with activated carbon and are convinced that these suits – from Scent-Lok, Robinson Labs, 10X and Walls – do

As you climb higher, your scent plume wafts further away from your immediate shooting lanes.

work as advertised. Because so much body heat and odor escapes from the hands, head and face, the suit manufacturers have recently accessorized their lines with masks, hoods, gloves and breath shields. The manufacturers also encourage suit owners to keep suits that are not in use in special storage sacks.

Are all the efforts to control scent worth the time, work and cost? I think they are if you remember the 10,000-to-one ratio, and I believe that if you were serious about making a commitment to take only mature big-game animals, you would do well to consider the advantages of an activated carbon suit. And what about the old stand-bys, the scents, lures and scent eliminating sprays? These all have a place in the hunters bag of tricks. Some lures will sometimes pique the curiosity of deer and other critters, but as we learn more about deer biology, the scents designed primarily to mask human odor have a more questionable future. If you choose to use the bad-smelling juices in the tiny brown bottles, remember to keep them away from your body, clothes and gear. A good spraying with a quality name-brand scent eliminator – into your hat, over your equipment and certainly to your boots – is one of my priorities during the final moments before I head to a stand.

Personally, I religiously wear carbon-lined clothing for hunting. I've learned to minimize my odor by not only wearing an outer garment lined with carbon, but by also wearing an undergarment or liner system as well. This practically doubles the effectiveness of the carbon, and based on many experiences in the field, I am absolutely convinced that these suits greatly enhance my ability to hunt undetected.

Wind and Odor

Thermal winds affect an animal's ability to detect a hunter's odor. Thermals are determined by the temperature and stability of the air. Warm air rises because it is less dense than cold air. Cold air is, therefore, denser or heavier, and it descends. In the early hours of morning, the air warms faster than the earth. The opposite is true in the evening, as air cools faster than the earth. All things being equal, air rises in the morning as it warms and descends in the evening as it cools.

This equation may be more noticeable when you are hunting terrain with some elevation to it such as mountains or steep river breaks. I hunted with Illinois Monster Bucks Outfitting Service in 1999, and we were successful by hunting with thermals in mind. We set up a location on top of an oak ridge over a farmed river bottom and waited for deer to run up from the bottom to the ridge for bedding. Just after sunup, when my scent began to rise with the thermals, deer began moving up the ridge toward our stand. The thermals provided excellent scent cover, and within an hour, I arrowed a fine buck.

There are many controversies about the best techniques in deer hunting. Most of them will always be a matter for friendly argument. What is the best caliber rifle for deer in brush country? Do mechanical or fixed-blade heads penetrate best? Do moon phases really affect deer behavior and movement? One thing all hunters agree on, however, is that wind plays a role in choosing a hunting stand and, I would argue, even choosing whether or not to hunt on a particular day.

While wind speed definitely affects deer, some air movement works to a deer's advantage. A light breeze brings it odors from farther away than it would normally detect without physically moving in their direction. The relatively regular pattern of leaf and grass movement in a breeze is easy for a deer to assess.

Strong or gusting winds are different. They cause branches and debris to flutter about unexpectedly. They confuse scent paths and cause odors to dissipate more rapidly. When the woods are in motion, there is excessive noise, which makes it difficult for deer to segregate and identify the noise it associates with predation.

So while increasing winds seem to favor the hunter, the opposite is actually true. The higher the wind, the spookier deer become. Apparently deer instincts tell them that the greater the scent confusion and the more unexpected the sound and movement in the environment, the greater their chances of surviving the day by staying in bed. My deduction is that on exceptionally windy days, you should complete some of those "honey-do" projects and save your "going-hunting" chips for better weather.

Michigan Buck

Whatever weapon you are using to kill deer ("tool you are using to harvest deer"), camouflage is an extremely important concept. Here is an example. One of my personal "hotspots" that is not far from where I live in Michigan is on the outskirts of a well-populated town. A nearby river sets the tone for this little slice of God's earth with planted fields west of a hardwoods funnel that leads to a swamp. Deer bed in the swamp and use the funnel through the hardwoods to reach the open fields. The problem to overcome in this spot is that the hardwoods are mostly tall and limbless for the initial 30 or 40 feet of trunk. This creates a situation where my stand is wide open and easy for deer to detect. It calls for extreme patience on stand, with no scratching or squirming, and a very careful camo selection.

Several years ago, I hunted this hotspot in a wind that was not very favorable. I wore a Scent-Lok suit with activated carbon and sprayed thoroughly with an odor eliminator, so I was confident that I could overcome the wind.

Look for mast-bearing trees like white oaks because when the acorns drop, the deer will appear.

Prior to climbing into my stand, I placed canisters of Tink's Doe-In-Heat Urine, a popular lure from Wellington, around the perimeter of my location. The first buck I noticed seemed to wind me. He turned and cautiously backtracked into the bed area and then it seemed to me that he caught a whiff of the attractant. For a moment, he acted as if he were torn between checking out the Doe-in-Heat and running for his life. Finally, he made up his mind and began walking in my direction again, knowing, I think, full well that a human was present and there was danger. I softly grunted. The buck looked right up at me, and I tried to freeze as tight as a marble statue. My Realtree camo blended perfectly with my background, which, from the deer's position on the floor of the woods, must have been pretty indistinct for angles and contrast against the gray sky. Within seconds, the deer lowered its head and continued walking toward the scent markers I had put out. I called a spine shot to my cameraman and then put a GameTracker Tri-Loc broadhead between the shoulder blades of the Michigan buck. The deer dropped in its tracks, and I credit the camo and the Doe-In-Heat attractant as much as my shot. So, whatever path you choose, you gotta believe!

Treestands

Every hunting opportunity requires a different solution, and that is what makes whitetail hunting such an exciting challenge. When you are away from the comfort of your soft, familiar armchair, almost anything can happen and sometimes does. You have to mentally move from the "entertain me" eyes-wide-shut television and computer-game zone to the living-wide-awake zone of the predator. Imagine how meaningful any hunting opportunity would become if you and your family actually depended on the meat you killed and brought home. One of the primary rules of success is versatility.

Choosing the right type of treestand is one of your most important equipment choices. There are more options than just buying a climber like everyone else in your hunting group has and then finding a straight tree to hike up with it. Fortunately, manufacturers have realized that a treestand must do more than allow you to get off the ground to hunt. Today's stands are quiet, strong, safe, light, versatile and, equally important, comfortable. Understanding and making effective use of these treestand advantages will make you a better hunter.

Climbing stands may offer the most versatility of any stand style. With a climber, you can hunt and scout at the same time. Equipped with backpack straps, a climber allows you to set up in fresh locations quietly and quickly.

One of the drawbacks to climbers is the width of the arms and the adjustable back-bar that encircles a tree and holds you securely off the ground. This width is about 2 feet.

Every time you loose an arrow or pull the trigger, Tim says, imagine that you are taking aim at the largest trophy deer you have ever seen. Imagine the deer's pumping heart and your arrow slicing through clean for a quick kill. Not practice – predation.

Fixed-position stands let you use practically any tree for an ambush site. If you hunt one secure area continually, fixed-position stands are ideal. You can put one up and leave it up or perhaps leave up its mounting bracket for the duration of the season.

A seasoned hunter who uses fixed-position stands will prepare several sites prior to the season. To keep the sites fresh and devoid of predictability, you can implement a "musical chair" approach. This lets you hunt stands on a rotation basis or change your plans quickly according to the weather.

Although the initial placement of a fixed-position stand is noisy, once it is hung, you can slip into the woods and up onto one of these stands quickly and quietly. The disadvantages of a fixed stand is that you need more gear for set-up, and it can take some time to put up the steps or ladder and haul up your gear. Quite a few states and many private landowners refuse to allow you to damage trees with screw-in steps. In this case, strap-on steps or a bulkier and more visible sectional ladder is necessary. Of course, using these means you will probably have to carry them into and out of the woods each time.

Ladder stands maximize safety and ease. Ladders are safer to enter and exit than any other type stand and are ideal for the novice or the physically challenged hunter. Many people are apprehensive, with good reason, about climbing trees and hunting from heights. In these cases, ladder stands (or ground blinds) are the best solution.

If ladder stands have disadvantages, they include difficulty of concealment and reduced mobility and versatility. Generally, these stands have lower platforms and are awkward to install alone. I have found ladders to be most useful in brushy conifers and areas where the vegetation is thick.

Permanent stands, fixed to trees with hammer and nail, are a thing of the past. There is little advantage except that you can make them larger. On the other hand, the profile of these large permanent stands is much greater, and the hunter is more easily detected than in smaller, lighter moveable stands. Repositioning is impossible, too. Building permanent stands is a huge problem as one must carry equipment and supplies, including hammers and saws into the woods. Ultimately, permanent stands are terrible safety hazards because as they age, they fall apart quickly. Finally, the remains of permanent stands are dead giveaways to excellent hunting spots.

In the fall of 1998, I went to Wisconsin for a grouse hunt. Grouse hunting is best when you hunt mornings with a dog. I opted to take my bow and hunt whitetails in the evening. The outfitter had erected ladder stands for the cameraman and me in a strip of hardwoods between a tag alder swamp and an alfalfa field.

Moments after we climbed into our stands, I realized our setup was off the mark. We were at least 30 yards shy of the ideal spot. Just out of bow range to our west was the remains of a permanent stand that was now falling apart. That was where we should have been. We stayed put for a while, but only a couple hours into the hunt, we saw an 8-pointer en route to the alfalfa meadow. Out of bow range, it eventually walked directly beneath the old permanent stand!

When you are climbing trees and hanging out 20 to 30 feet off the ground, you have to keep one part of your mind focused on safety. I absolutely believe you must use a full body harness when you are putting up a stand, when you are climbing up or down and while you are hunting. Today, we know that a simple waist belt or chest harness won't do. If you fall while you are using a waist belt, you can end up hanging from the stand with serious spinal injuries, and a chest harness can make it almost impossible to climb back onto your stand.

Of course, the first rule of hunting is to hunt with a partner or to make sure that some significant other knows where you are going and when you expect to return. When you are treestand hunting, this is especially important because each year thousands of hunters fall and hundreds end the season with life-altering injuries.

While whitetails do look up, they don't walk around with their heads cocked permanently gazing upward watching for you. It just seems that way. By elevating yourself above the animal's peripheral vision you significantly reduce your chance of being detected. Remember what the University of Georgia's Dr. Karl Miller said about deer apparently seeing a broad band rather than a spot. They may see peripherally above and below that band rather than, like humans, to the extreme sides.

Most archers hang stands between 12 and 15 feet high. The degree of concealment at such heights is marginal. A whitetail can easily detect you at that elevation. Experience says a deer's normal field of view extends upward more than 15 feet.

By hunting at about 25 feet, you sharply reduce the odds of being seen. This height also helps remove your scent from the immediate area or within bow range. (In theory, gravity brings odor molecules, which are heavier than air, down to ground level. With constant air movement, the higher your elevation, the farther your scent plume travels before falling to the ground.)

Hunting above 25 feet may adversely affect arrow trajectory though. At these heights, hunters tend to dip the bow-arm shoulder, thereby changing their anchor, although with a release and a peep this may no longer be as crucial as it was when most archers were finger shooters. Nevertheless, dipping one's shoulder is preventable by bending at the waist. This keeps your shoulders horizontal and in the same plane to the bow as when you are practicing. The higher you go, the more practice you need shooting from that height.

Now, I believe that trimming branches or small trees out of shooting lanes around stands is highly problematic. It is not possible to shoot an arrow through a screen of brush and hit your target. A single leaf can be enough to send your arrow sailing off course. So, many hunters clear lanes obsessively, and this is dangerous when it happens too close to the opening of the season because deer will change their patterns or be extra-wary in the area.

Frankly, I do not believe in cutting shooting lanes. Yes, you may have to remove a couple limbs that prevent you from climbing the tree, but when you begin trimming in the woods, every view changes – yours and the deer's – and that cannot be good. Your goal is to exert the least pressure and achieve the greatest result.

When it comes to placing stands, the most common mistake we make is holding out for the "perfect tree" rather than the "right tree." The perfect tree is the tree in the best possible shooting location. The right tree gives you advantages that will allow you to take a mature animal. The right tree is not located directly on top of the animal's travel route. The right tree is in a downwind position in a setup offering background cover such as is found in fir trees and oaks.

Background cover is of utmost importance because it reduces the odds that a deer will see you. Firs give you the most cover, but when they are not present, I like a tree with numerous mini-trunks or big branches below and around me. They help disguise my profile. When multi-trunk trees aren't available, I cut foliage from down the trail and knit it into and around my stand.

Most hunters do not realize how little pressure it takes to move a buck out of its core area. There is never a time when a deer's nose is off duty. Every deer understands that his nose is more foolproof than his eyes or ears. Out of curiosity, I think, I have had deer approach watchfully from upwind when I know they saw something unusual (me) move, but in my experience, a single sniff of human odor will send deer racing away. And this, of course, reinforces the first rule of stand placement: put yourself downwind of where you expect to shoot a deer.

Determining the downwind side of a deer trail is usually easy. In most places, there is a prevailing wind direction during deer season. Westerly and southerly winds are common in much of the midwestern, eastern and southeastern parts of the country. As cold fronts move through, winds usually shift abruptly and flow from the northwest or north. Within a few days, winds rotate clockwise and resume their more common southern or western flow.

While this general pattern applies on a regional basis, wind direction in your hunting area will certainly vary. Mountainous terrain produces unique wind patterns that may differ sharply, even from one hillside to the next. So study the wind pattern in your area, and place your stand accordingly.

Many hunters I know like to set up their stands early, but some of them will be unusable when the wind is wrong. If an area is particularly hot and you want to hunt there regardless of wind, hang one or two additional stands that can be downwind when the wind shifts direction. Because approaching weather fronts cause deer to be active, I sit in one stand prior to the arrival of a cold front and plan to switch to a different stand as the wind changes. I have a rule of thumb that says if I am really serious about a spot, I will hang six fixed-position stands per 100 acres of hunting territory: one for each primary wind direction and two extras to prevent over-hunting a particular spot.

Sunrise and sunset can be the best or worst of times. When the sun glares over your back and floods the area you are expecting to see deer, you are sitting pretty. If the wind is in your face and you are still, there is little chance a whitetail will know you are nearby. If the sun glares into your face, however, you may as well climb down because you cannot shoot what you cannot see.

I have sat in stands that positioned me to shoot deer that could only see me by staring directly into the blinding glare of a low sun. It was almost too easy. I have also sat on stands when the sun worked against me. Not only could I not see the deer, my movements were extremely easy to detect. If I can't have the sun at my back, I make sure it's to my side. Set up with the sun at your side and you can usually use the location both late and early.

Position your treestand for every possible advantage. This means more than positioning yourself within range of a trail or spiderweb crossing. It means setting up a favorable shot long before any deer comes by.

While no hunter can predict with certainty where deer will appear, we all make informed guesses. Knowing the direction deer will travel as they move past allows you to position your stand for maximum advantage. Let's say a north-south deer trail runs 20 yards west of your stand. If the majority of tracks are headed north or if most buck rubs are on the south side of area trees, assume that deer travel past you in a left-to-right direction. A right-handed archer should place his stand to face north. This sets up broadside and quartering-away shots. The worst place to hang your stand would be on the south side of the tree. You would have to stand and face the tree to shoot, and you would have to draw before the deer moves broadside, increasing your chances of being spotted.

On Hunting From The Ground

Trying to kill a deer from the ground is risky business. The key to ground hunting is adaptability, and this means learning about pits, stalking, still-hunting, ground blinds and drives.

Not many 8-pointers would score better than this wide-racked whitetail with thick bases and only the tiniest spurs for deductions.

Even today there is value in understanding pit blinds and how to make them work in scenarios that don't offer treestand setups. Hunters have used pit blinds to take pronghorns around waterholes for years, and there is absolutely no reason this tactic can't work on whitetails.

Whether you choose or are forced into a pit blind, it has to be properly dug and positioned as carefully as a treestand. Fencerows adjacent to well-used deer trails provide ideal places for pit blinds. Other places include weed patches, sloughs or creeks and, where the landowner permits, the edges of agricultural fields.

Pit blinds are awfully hard to dig, so plan before you begin. You want a pit to be spacious, but that means more digging. You want it to be comfortable and that's even more digging! Still, if you are going to do this, when the time comes, all you want to have to do is pick up your bow, draw and shoot. You do not want to have to worry about such things as remembering to lean backward or whether your bow will clear the edge of the pit.

I suggest you dig the pit at least 3 feet deep by 5 feet long and 4 feet wide. Set a bench or chair snugly against the back wall for comfort. (This is a lot of earth moving, so select your site well!)

All pit blinds require cover because as much as we suspect deer look up, we know these animals look down. Background matters most, so position your blind in the shade if possible, even though this probably means you will run into one helluva lot of roots. You may even want to plant or transplant permanent cover around the edges. While the initial effort to build a pit blind is considerable, a good one could last for years.

Other than a treestand, ground blinds are the most effective means to get after a big deer. Their greatest advantages are mobility and diversity of style. Generally, little or no assembly is required. Blinds are lightweight and water and wind resistant. They are also offered in a variety of camo patterns and most have shoot-through window mesh that will not affect the flight of an arrow.

Hunting behind a couple hay bales can work in open fields. These heavy bales need to be positioned by the farmer before the season so deer become accustomed to them. Hay-bale hunting is effective in fields of alfalfa or clover where large bales are common. Bring a stool to sit on and be prepared to listen for deer on the opposite side of the large bales, the side you cannot see without exposing yourself.

When you want out of your blind, and we all do every now and then, still-hunting is appealing, but it requires a huge amount of patience. Each step taken in the woods opens a new view. Success comes when you learn to slow down each movement and study the forest before you move forward. Still-hunters learn to evaluate each shadow and object and take more time than they ever imagined would be needed to move through a woodlot. Of course, the first rule of still-hunting is to make sure the wind is in your face!

Several years ago, I hunted the edge of a cornfield. Wearing one of Bob Walker's Game Ear hearing aids, I could actually hear deer stripping the corn, and from my stand, I could see the tops of waving corn tassels. This allowed me to make a rough estimation of where the deer were. I climbed down and slipped into the corn.

Because I am tall, I could stalk through the corn and watch for swaying tassels. Within a few minutes, I saw a deer tine. Careful to stay to the buck's backside, I slid the bow between two stalks of corn, quietly drew, adjusted to the leaves against my face and sent an AFC Game Tracker arrow into the buck's boiler room.

Tim grunted and killed this fine buck at Jeff Kent's Ranch in Texas.

Top: *Game Tracker's pop-up blinds set up fast.*

Middle: *Even minimal effort camouflaging this Game Tracker blind makes a huge and very positive difference in breaking up its outline.*

Bottom: *Four quick steps to putting up a portable ground blind. If you wear a suit of activated carbon when you hunt inside one of these, you are not only quickly camouflaged, you are also almost invisible!*

The Deer Drive

Although deer drives have been out of favor for 25 years, they can be productive. The operative words are patience and synchronization. Drives succeed when they are carefully planned and executed. Quality, not speed. Rushing to the end of a drive is novice behavior, and it allows mature animals to slip out the sides or even double back and escape. The challenge is to keep the drivers in line and have your best shots and coolest hands as standers. It's one of the few team things we deer hunters do in the field.

For a drive to work, it is especially helpful to know the terrain so that you can anticipate which way deer will move when they are disturbed. If you are only guessing about the area before a drive, you reduce your chance of success and increase the chance that someone will get hurt. Sound shots are NEVER recommended for a deer drive or any other time for that matter.

- Make sure someone is "drivemaster" and everyone else knows he or she is in charge. This person should be the one with greatest knowledge of the terrain and deer patterns. Use a map or aerial photo to orient participants and then synchronize watches before moving to starting positions.

- Keep the number of hunters manageable. Large groups are difficult to coordinate, and it seems there is always that one egocentric person who refuses to accept direction.

- Driving huge tracts of woods takes too much time and gives deer too many escape routes. Keep the area relatively small. A football-field-size plot is about right.

- Always use flankers, drivers who work the outside edges and who can spot fleeing deer.

- Stand hunters at the end of the drive should be elevated so they can look down into cover and watch for deer slipping through the brush ahead of the drivers.

- When planning a drive, take the wind direction into account. It's better to have deer smell the drivers than the standers.

- Shots will ordinarily be at moving deer, so put your best shooters on stand.

- Safety should be your paramount concern, as driving deer is fraught with danger to hunters as well as deer. Wear plenty of blaze orange! Because drivers sometimes get shots at deer, a driver should make every effort to stay in visual contact with drivers to the left and right. No driver should take a shot to the immediate left or right.

- Drivers must be sensitive to what's happening behind them. Often, a buck will remain bedded and let the drivers pass before it bolts in the opposite direction.

- Sometimes, in thick cover, a second drive will scare up bedded bucks.

- Try "backstanding," positioning a couple hunters at the initial take-off point for drivers. Often bucks will slip between drivers and filter out the back of the drive.

- Small pieces of isolated cover hold deer! Use natural barriers such as cliffs or riverbanks to your advantage and to limit a deer's escape possibilities.

- If a hunter takes a shot, he should mark the spot with something large, bright and highly visible and continue with the drive. He should not stop and begin to track the deer. Otherwise, the line becomes uncoordinated and guaranteeing the safety of others becomes impossible.

- Windy days are excellent for drives. Deer will not naturally move much when the wind is blowing hard, and they should be easier to scare up from their beds.

- Loud, raucous, pincer-like movements with the drivers whistling and shouting make life difficult for stand hunters to score because deer panic and race by too quickly to make accurate shots. This is especially the case with archers. Silent drives push animals in predetermined directions with deer slowly sneaking away and offering easier targets.

A Hunt During The Breeding Period

Much is written about the rut. Many of us hunters depend on the fact that a whitetail buck acts differently when it is looking for a girlfriend than it does "normally" or when it is unaware of danger. The words "stupid" and "possessed" describe how single-minded bucks seem to become during this brief period each year. Their careless behavior helps put the odds in your favor.

Whitetails vocalize to communicate, but this seems secondary. They primarily communicate with glandular secretions, requiring the olfactory senses to interpret them. A prime example is called "flehmin," for a buck's behavior when it detects the scent of a doe near her 30 to 40 hour receptivity. The buck lifts its head and curls its upper lip up over its nostrils. This lets scent molecules adhere to the surface of the nasal passage, sending a message to the brain and allowing the buck to determine the doe's estrous status. This complex signaling is only one of many communications deer use during the rut.

A quality estrous deer lure can be an effective aid in killing a mature buck during the rut and pre-rut. Now, I said "aid." Lures and deer urine are only tools, because the most important issue is your hunting location. A lure must be placed where the buck has a chance to acquire the aroma and you can get a shot.

In this excerpt from Tim's conversation with Dr. Karl Miller, a deer biologist from the University of Georgia, Tim learns more about what scientists have discovered about how deer communicate using their various glands and bodily secretions, crucial things to know when hunting the rut.

The Tarsal Gland

Tim: Hunters have long believed that there is a special property in urine that allows deer to communicate. Is this true?

Dr. Miller: It looks like a variety of glands may be involved in deer recognition and communication. Deer urine has a special place in this system because it works with the tarsal glands, and if you have been observant in the field, you have probably seen deer sniff each other's tarsals.

Throughout the year, bucks, and does to a lesser extent, rub urinate down their legs, flooding their tarsal glands with urine. The tarsals are tufts of long hairs associated with a gland on each leg. These glands secrete a fatty material that coats the hairs, and within this warm, wet, fatty environment live several dozen types of bacteria. The bacteria change compounds in deer urine to many purposes. One of the by-products is odor. We have identified 103 separate volatile compounds in the tarsal tufts of bucks.

According to Jon Gassett and Karen Alexy, different complexes of bacteria inhabit the tarsal glands of different individual deer and these complexes give them individual smells. We believe that deer use these smells to identify one another. Apparently, does recognize their fawns this way and some complexes are more prevalent in dominant than non-dominant individuals!

An interesting realization is that deer produce their individual odors in the same way human under-arm odor is produced, although we don't urinate in our armpits.

Deer droppings. Although it is easy to assess their freshness and hence how long ago a deer stood in the spot, droppings do not tell the casual observer anything significant other than that a deer has been through the area.

Tim: So, a fresh tarsal gland could be a useful hunting tool. Kind of like a deer lure.

Dr. Miller: Well, yes, but there's no telling what that gland will be saying to the deer that smells it. It may carry a challenging odor or could be from a dominant individual and frighten deer away from you. I think using a tarsal scent will likely be most effective during the two to three weeks just prior to the peak of the rut when scraping activity is at a peak.

Additional studies we have conducted indicate that the female reproductive tract is the primary source of reproductive chemical communication in deer. Vaginal secretions from estrous females, rather than urine, are apparently the source of sexually attractive odors. Our next step is to understand whether urine carries any of the chemical signals produced in the deer's reproductive tract.

Not long ago, I was hunting with my friend Steve Shoop at his place in Iowa. Steve's J&S Trophy Hunts has operations in Iowa and Missouri. One of the other hunters asked whether I knew if the spot we were hunting was any good.

"What did Steve say?" I asked.

The fellow replied, "Steve said during the rut, the deer just like to use that spot. When they are rutting, they specifically travel through that area."

"That's good enough for me," I said.

The rut causes bucks to move in unusual patterns. They may use some of the same highways as when food was the primary stimulus, but when does become their number one focus, in most cases the patterns change. All things being equal, bucks will follow the same routes year after year.

Steve knew that. Since he was a boy, many bruisers had been taken from that spot. The location had classic topographical advantages including a long, dominant ridge of hardwoods with treestands positioned on a gentle saddle feeding into a perpendicular draw and also feeding into the other side of the main ridge.

Bob Fenton, a hunter from Pennsylvania, had taken a 150-class buck there a week earlier. From what I could determine during our first day on stand, I knew it would only be a short time before another good buck would expose itself. The count at the end of the second day was 13 bucks and six does, including a 130-class 8-pointer with an 8-inch pair of brow tines! Practically a shooter.

The third day was a hunter's dream! Clear with light winds. Temperatures in the low 20's and a heavy frost. With the rut near its peak, I placed several scent bombs around my stand to saturate the air. Even though morning thermals were carrying most scent upward, there were still two of us in the tree (a cameraman and myself), as this hunt would be captured on film for my television show.

Soon the sun would be high enough to stir up a breeze. The way things had been going, there was a chance that a mature buck could come from any direction.

Soon, a lone doe trotted left to right in the draw below. She bolted out of sight when a flash of sunlight glinted off massive bone betwixt the brush and a cedar behind her. A moment was all it took for two deer to exit the thicket. They headed up the right side of the small draw, the huge buck in pursuit. I panicked because I thought the doe was taking the buck with her over the main ridge to the other side! Because they were a good 70 yards out, I did not have a shot. The buck then flanked the doe, cutting her off and turning her in a direction that put them underneath our stand. As the

This kind of portable ground blind sets up in less than a minute and allows you to quickly respond to wind and weather conditions.

doe ran by within 15 yards, I used my natural voice to try to bleat them to a halt. They did not even slow down.

With the doe standing 80 yards away with the buck right behind her, I let down from full draw. The deer looked back up the hill from where they had come and tried to figure out what the funny sound had been and where it came from. That was a heart breaker. We got the event on film, and looking back at the footage, I figured the buck would have easily scored in the 150+ class.

The two deer milled around on the left slope of the draw, and now and then, we got a glimpse of feet or antler as the doe fed on acorns and the buck stood guard.

My eyes were locked on the two deer when I heard my cameraman hiss, "Behind you!" Two bucks. Indeed, two good bucks were walking through the shallow dip and headed down the draw behind us. I don't remember if the Booner was still tending his doe, but I was still thinking about him as I turned around to take my first peek at the newcomers. The lead buck was the biggest, and as I added up horn length, I cut loose a moment of foolishness when I asked aloud, "Should I take him?"

"I'm rolling," the cameraman said.

When I turned to look at the deer, my feet were in the proper position and my release was already on the bowstring. The big buck was only 15 yards away. I needed a diversion to draw the bow without alerting it. Either buck could easily nail us if we made a bad move.

Then the scent bombs around the stand came to our rescue. The smaller buck, no slouch at about 120 P&Y, was testing the air and lip curling, letting the strong aroma take him to la-la land. I had also placed a few squirts of gel-based Tink's 69 on the trunks of a couple saplings that were right in front of him. The 140-class bruiser now turned his head back, giving me my chance. In one motion I drew, anchored and drove the First-Cut Magnum into his ribcage and out behind the knuckle of his right shoulder.

It was a very short walk to the beautiful 10-point and the culmination of an exciting day. The kill was the means to an end, a happy end.

So, as you are learning techniques to stack the odds in your favor, understanding the rut is a quintessential factor in becoming an accomplished whitetail hunter.

Chapter 14

Attitude:
Preparation And Predation

Our sport, hunting, is deficient in one area: attitude. To prove my assertion, I would first of all suggest that we are afraid to call hunting a sport, probably because we kill animals. Somehow, after the Holocaust and Saddam and Pol Pot and Rwanda, linking the word "sport" with killing one of God's creatures pushes us, mentally at least, toward the abyss. So, we hem and haw about hunting being a passion or a tradition or a "way of life."

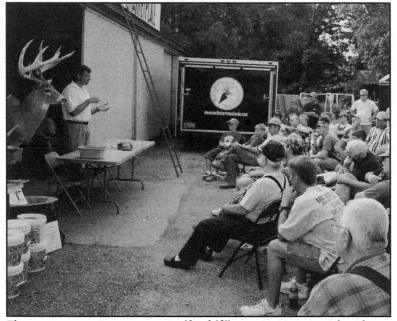

There are many ways to prepare yourself to fulfill your commitment to take only mature big game. Expand your idea of scouting to include attending seminars, taking aerial photos and interviewing taxidermists, not just the old-fashioned boots-on-the-ground study of the terrain.

(No one calls bowhunting a "hobby," as that makes it seem too nerdy, too much like stamp collecting or model airplane building. Target archery can be a hobby, but not hunting.) There is nothing wrong with "way of life," except that we think of farming or fishing for a living, for instance, as a way of life. Those professions are all-encompassing. They are profession-based and leave their distinctiveness on the balance of one's life.

How many times have you read that we "harvest" or that we "take" big game? "Edgar harvested the new world record." We harvest grain. We take a bite. Baloney. We kill and eat. If you are going to be an efficient and deadly predator – and you are – you are going to have to be clear about what you are doing. You are going to become the most skilled and efficient killer on the planet, and you are handicapping yourself by shooting the bow and arrow rather than a scoped high-power rifle. You have to get some attitude to go along with our sport's self-imposed meekness and humility. You are a killer, not a "harvester" or a "taker." If *Ladies Home Journal* interviews you about bowhunting, by all means, be a "harvester." Otherwise, stay focused.

This is what I mean by attitude. To move forward in a crowded century that has little patience for the virtues that we learn by hunting, virtues like craftsmanship and respect, we hunters are going to have to lose our fear of not being politically correct. Now, I don't suggest that we put a "Happiness Is A Warm Gut Pile" bumper sticker on our cars, NOT AT ALL, but I do suggest that we stop apologizing for being hunters, for killing God's creatures. Sharks kill God's creatures. Tyrannosaurus rex killed God's creatures. Lions kill God's creatures, and there is evidence that they sometimes kill simply because it is fun. God kills God's creatures! They were or are all predators, like us. And who is to say that they were any more or less "natural creatures" than homo sapiens? They kill. They eat. End of story. Stop apologizing.

Several years ago, I was preparing to sell a house and was interviewing prospective realtors. One of them told me that I would have to remove the big-game heads from the walls so they did not offend a potential purchaser. I did not hire her. I did not take the heads down; the house sold just fine.

I am tired of apologizing and weaseling around the fact that I am a hunter who kills animals. I am totally exhausted with "industry associations" (primarily groups of manufacturers who are operated by bookkeepers and model-airplane builders who make their living selling us stuff) rewriting the language I use to describe my joy in hunting a trophy deer, killing it, eating it and mounting its head and antlers on my wall. If you are going to make a serious commitment to killing only mature big-game animals, you are soon going to be a very good hunter. You are elevating yourself from scavenger, the hyena or wild dog or association status, to the predator status of the leopard and the cheetah. The lion does not apologize for killing a wildebeest and feeding its family. The lion does not want to buy any more Made-In-China trinkets or buy at any more BoxMarts. It's time to push away the individuals and groups who want to put us in the closet. Apparently, no one likes it in there.

Shooting downhill at 3-D deer. Forget practice, Tim says. Think of this only as preparation for the moment of truth.

Never Practice Again!

Take your new attitude and vow that you will never practice again. Refuse to practice. You are not in the marching band; you are not a member of the choir or learning card tricks. Practice is for target shooters, basketball players and politicians.

Never practice again. Prepare. Get an attitude and kill big deer. The first step is imagining that you can do it. You can. Now, get busy!

Forget your mom nagging you about practicing the piano. Forget all that "practice makes perfect" stuff and today's chic spin-off, "perfect practice makes perfect." Forget what the old ball coach used to growl about people playing the game the same way they practice: practice hard and you'll play hard. That's bull do-do and you have always known it. You knew it then. You were just powerless to say so. What they should have told you was to get your game on, get your attitude on.

Preparing to kill a big-game animal begins upstairs in your brain, not downstairs in your wallet or even your hand-eye coordination. I want you to reprogram your thinking away from the idea of "practice" and toward the idea of predation, killing something. Practice and the "love of the game" are for amateurs and sports announcers. I want you to steer clear of people who say that hunting is so much more than just taking the life of a critter. Avoid hunters who claim that the essence of the hunt is in a frosty sunrise, in the fog sneaking through the trees or in the camaraderie of a deer camp. Fog is for losers and deer camps are for old men. You are preparing to find and kill something enormous. Screw the fog. Focus. You are not going to be a loser, not ever.

You do not need to practice. You need to prepare … with purpose.

Although we have left it until the end of the book, Step Number One is mental preparation, and it begins in your living room or your den. Why not take the family for a walk-through? Prepare them for clearing out the bowling trophies and grocery store art prints, because you are going to need the space to hang some big, trophy-class deer. If they understand your commitment to hunting, this is a natural follow-through. Does it put you on the spot for nagging if you are not immediately successful? Of course it does. Do not worry about it. You will be successful.

All the talk about "visualization" since the hippie days of the '60s and the awareness that Zen consciousness wasn't available only to Japanese samurai warriors will do you good here. Practice implies that we are trying to tune up our bow and make our arrows fly smoothly into an 8-inch pie plate. Practice suggests that we have intermediate goals. I suggest that you prepare with only one goal, killing a big deer every time you even think about hunting. Every time you touch your bow, every time you climb your treestand in the backyard and shoot at the 3-D target and the paper you have scattered around the yard, imagine that you are flying your arrow into the heart of your deer. Your deer. Know that you are killing a huge deer, one that will grace your family living room for generations.

Ban the word "practice" from your hunting vocabulary and replace it with the Boy Scout motto: Be Prepared. You may be flying your arrow into a pie plate, but it is not a pie plate. It is the heart of your commitment. This is not nitpicking. This is a change of awareness, a fundamental change in your attitude; and I do want you to get some attitude.

Whatever religion you practice, one of the tenets is that if you believe, it will happen. "Build it and they will come" or "When you are ready, the master will appear" are just variations of the Boy Scout attitude.

We're not just talking about believing in general. We are talking about belief based on commitment and part of that commitment is that you are going to have your gear in first-class condition. You will be able to nail an 8-inch paper plate with a broadhead consistently at 50 yards. Believing in yourself makes it happen.

Tim took this mule deer by paying careful attention to buck travel routes and then actively moving to intercept it.

Passive To Active

I am telling you the truth. This stuff works.

There is ample evidence in the pre-historic record that when early man began to interact with his environment, he began to evolve rapidly. At some point, early man recognized the earth was more than something to walk on or lie down on. At some point, an early Einstein realized that he could pick up a stone and use it as a tool. Later, one of his ancestors realized that he could fashion it as a cutting and killing instrument. The move was from passive to active, and that is just the kind of move you are going to make if you choose to commit yourself to taking only mature big-game animals.

Apparently, our early proto-ancestors were on the earth for several million years before it occurred to one of them to pick up a stick to defend itself. When humans began to defend themselves, striking back rather than just running and hiding or climbing a tree, something changed in their brain. Immediately, I believe, they joined the family of predators; immediately they recognized that they could stalk and kill their food. Their confidence eventually encompassed giant wooly mammoths, the largest mammals ever to walk the earth, twice as large as African bull elephants.

You are doing exactly the same thing that those early humans did, and you are going to have the same results. You are going to apply yourself to your commitment, and the biofeedback is going to change you in a far shorter period than a few million years. You are going to evolve from a passive hunter to an active predator who is fully engaged in hunting. You are going to learn how to apply in the field all the tricks we modern hunters know and the solutions to many of hunting's riddles. In a few years, you will have racks on the wall to attest to your evolution.

Practice is a passive activity. Predation is an act of aggression. However, if you are one of those individuals who just can't change, give yourself permission to say that your task is to "Practice With Purpose." And I hope it works for you.

I feel it necessary to make one brief and perhaps unnecessary announcement. By "getting your attitude on," I do not mean that you should spread your field-dressed deer on the hood of your pick-up and parade it back and forth in front of the local anti-hunter's home. You cannot change or control that person. I am suggesting that you get totally focused on what you can control, yourself. Please exercise your very best judgment and common sense.

Never Quit

I want to end with a little story about everything going wrong. Well, not everything, but enough, especially when the trophy is a wild turkey.

Never quit. That sounds like my old college football coach at Western Kentucky University. We knew we were not going to the Rose Bowl. No matter how good we were, we were a small school compared to UCLA or Michigan, but we had a lot of pride and really worked our butts off. Still, our sweating and lifting and hitting never seemed to satisfy coach. "Never give up, Hooey," he'd growl. "You're a quitter. Hit that man harder. You're not going to break and neither will he!" Coach was not someone who won you over with love, but as a linebacker, hitting somebody harder was my job. I loved playing football and I never quit on an assignment, so I took his name-calling personally and resented it until I heard him say exactly the same thing to the other linebackers. Then I realized what his point was. Not humiliation or punishment, but a stinging whip to make me a better football player.

Since I made my own commitment to take only mature big game, I have run into countless situations where deer and turkeys and elk have made a fool out of me, made me feel like giving up. I have even run into people who poked fun at me when I did not bring in wall-hanger buck.

Do you ever work terribly hard and still get "disrespected" with lousy results? Sure, it happens now and then. On the one hand, I understand that my satisfaction is internally driven and that as long as I hunt legally and ethically and prepare as thoughtfully as possible, what other people say is irrelevant to the outcome. If I allow my enjoyment of a hunt to be based on what other people say or do or write, then I turn my power over to them. That is not going to happen.

In spite of my commitment, hard work and conscious effort, I know there are going to be dry hunts when, for whatever reason, nothing turns up or, worse yet, I screw up a perfectly good opportunity. I have spent thousands of dollars on hunts when I did not get a shot … and had days when my arrow sped within inches of a beautiful, trophy deer that I could see on the dinner table and on the wall, all because I hurried my shot or chose the wrong pin. In these cases, recognize or acknowledge the missed opportunity and move on. If you are hunting consciously, you have to recognize that you are going to make mistakes and not be hard on yourself. As the Zen masters say, touch the pain with the feather of your thought and then let it go.

Several years ago, I was working on taking the Grand Slam of America's wild turkeys by bow. I had killed an Osceola in Florida, a Rio Grande

The payoff for making a commitment to taking only mature animals is the very real possibility that you will fulfill all of your hunting ambitions.

Flanked by his camera operators, Tim proudly displays a fine whitetail buck. Tim has never hunted in a preserve. All of his trophy game animals were taken in free-ranging conditions.

in Texas and a Merriams on the border of Wyoming and Montana, a place the local folks call "Wytana."

To hunt the Eastern gobbler, I drove to Centerville, Iowa, and met some friends from Knight Muzzleloader. I saw a ton of big Eastern gobblers, but I had a tough time getting one into range. Bad luck dogged every move. The one time I thought I was going to get a shot was on the third day. With a gobbler only 15 yards away, I placed my arrow perfectly in the middle of a tiny hanging vine. If that vine had not been precisely where it was, I would have scored instantly and could have gone home happy. The doggone turkey trotted off like it was not even concerned.

On my fourth and final day of the hunt, I went out in the morning and tried to owl up a bird. Nothing. We set up at several likely spots. Nothing. I was discouraged and in my mind began scrambling to make a back-up plan. Where could I go to finish the Grand Slam? What use was three-quarters of a Grand Slam?

Life is short, play hard, Tim says. If you wait to make the hunting commitment that you know is right for you ... well, you just may wait too long. Good luck and great hunting.

Then, in the ride back in the truck that afternoon, we saw a monster gobbler in a small cornfield bordering public land. On one side of this field was a long strip of woods with plenty of brushy cover, but when the gobbler heard our truck, he ran away into the woods. That bird was spooked. It was obvious that he had been hunted hard.

Because the area was public land, I hopped out of the truck right there, with just my bow and turkey vest, and took off on foot after the gobbler. For the first three birds of the Grand Slam, I hunted out of a Game Tracker blind and was concealed sufficiently to be prepared for almost anything. This was different. I was winging it, hunting by the seat of my pants, and the odds did not look good.

Since I knew where the turkey went into the woods, I stationed myself in the field right outside. I called a few times, and when I heard a gobbler spitting and drumming, I slipped quietly into the brush. I called again and this time heard the tom gobble on the opposite side of the woods. I kept calling and we kept getting closer.

It was late in the afternoon when I noticed an opening in the woods where an old pine had fallen. I decided to make a setup. The opening was about 6 feet deep and 15 yards across, and I felt certain of two things. One, that if that tom kept on its current course, it would walk through that very spot and two, because the brush was thick, it could not see me move from the sides.

Instead of making a big yelping call and backing off again, I did a soft purr, clucked and then trailed off. That turkey made quite a racket in the leaves running toward me. My heart raced. I called again, and it began drumming and came closer. It appeared right where I had predicted. The moment it strutted through the opening I was ready and let him have it through the chest. It was almost 2 hours from the moment I jumped out of the pickup and ran into the field without my blind or a plan.

That tom allowed me to complete my Grand Slam with a bow in 28 days. It was a biggie, with 1 1/4-inch spurs, an 11-inch beard and a weight of 27 pounds.

It was a wild turkey and not a whitetail buck, but the story illustrates what I mean about never giving up. I had been on the road for more than a month and was ready to be home. It was late in the day. I was bone tired and disappointed after hunting 4 days without success. And then I recognized an opportunity, even though at the time I probably thought of it as one final desperate chance. Chasing that bird on foot was a long shot. While it was not a foregone conclusion, everything worked out. That bird could have kept on making tracks away from me. It should have. But for me, a combination of luck and persistence paid off. Never quit. Coach was right.

APPENDIX

Appendix 1 – North American Wildlife Resource Departments

Although they are known by many different names, each state and province in North America has a department of natural resources or division of game and fish. If you are looking for an out-of-state hunting location for a mature deer or any other big-game animal, these departments or ministries, funded by your tax dollars, are a public resource that should not be overlooked. Their publications and Internet sites offer a diverse and immensely surprising volume of information, and they are continually being updated. (The information presented here was accurate as of January 2004.)

US State Agencies

Alabama Department of Conservation and Natural Resources, Division of Wildlife and Freshwater Fisheries, 64 N Union St., Suite 468, Montgomery, AL 36130 (334) 242-3465 www.dcnr.state.al.us

Alaska Department of Fish and Game, PO Box 25526, Juneau, AK 99802-5526 (907) 465-4100 www.state.ak.us/local/akpages/FISH.GAME

Arizona Game & Fish, 2221 W Greenway Rd., Phoenix, AZ 85023-4399 (602) 942-3000 www.gf.state.az.us

Arkansas Game and Fish Commission, 2 Natural Resources Dr., Little Rock, AR 72205 (800) 364-4263/(501) 223-6300 www.agfc.state.ar.us

California Department of Fish and Game, 1416 Ninth St., Sacramento, CA 95814 (916) 445-0411 www.dfg.ca.gov

Colorado Division of Wildlife, 6060 Broadway, Denver, CO 80216 (303) 297-1192 www.wildlife.state.co.us

Connecticut Department of Environmental Protection, Bureau of Natural Resources, 79 Elm St., Hartford, CT 06106-5127 (860) 424-3011 www.dep.state.ct.us

Delaware Department of Natural Resources and Environmental Control, Division of Fish and Wildlife, 89 King's Hwy., Dover, DE 19901 (302) 739-5295/4431 www.dnrec.state.de.us/fw

Florida Fish and Wildlife Conservation Commission, 620 S Meridian St., Farris Bryant Building, Tallahassee, FL 32399-1600 (888) 486-8356/(850) 488-4676 www.floridaconservation.org or www.myfwc.com

Georgia Department of Natural Resources, Wildlife Resources Division, Headquarters Office, 2070 US Hwy. 278 SE, Social Circle, GA 30025 (770) 918-6400/(888) 748-6887 www.georgiawildlife.dnr.state.ga.us

Hawaii Department of Land and Natural Resources, Kalanimoku Bldg., 1151 Punchbowl St., Honolulu, HI 96813 (808) 587-0400 www.hawaii.gov/dlnr

Idaho Fish and Game, 600 S Walnut/PO Box 25, Boise, ID 83707 (208) 334-3700 www.state.id.us/fishgame

Illinois Department of Natural Resources, One Natural Resources Way, Springfield, IL 62702-1271 (217) 782-9272/2965 www.dnr.state.il.us

Indiana Department of Natural Resources, Division of Fish and Wildlife, 402 W Washington St., Indianapolis, IN 46204 (317) 232-4080 www.in.gov/dnr/fishwild

Iowa Department of Natural Resources, Wildlife Bureau, 502 E 9th St., Des Moines, IA (515) 281-5918 www.iowadnr.com

Kansas Department of Wildlife and Parks, 1020 S Kansas, Topeka, KS 66612-1327 (785) 296-2281/(620) 672-5911 www.kdwp.state.ks.us

Kentucky Department of Fish and Wildlife, 1 Game Farm Road, Frankfort, KY 40601 (800) 858-1549 www.kdfwr.state.ky.us

Louisiana Department of Wildlife and Fisheries, 2000 Quail Drive, Baton Rouge, LA 70808 (225) 765-2800 www.wlf.state.la.us

Maine Department of Inland Fisheries and Wildlife, 284 State St., Augusta, ME 04333-0041 (207) 287-8000/8003 www.state.me.us/ifw

Maryland Department of Natural Resources, Wildlife and Heritage Service, Tawes State Office Building, E-1 580 Taylor Ave., Annapolis, MD 21401 (410) 260-8540 www.dnr.state.md.us/wildlife

Massachusetts Department of Fisheries, Wildlife and Environmental Law Enforcement, 251 Causeway St., Suite 400, Boston, MA 02114-2104 (413) 545-0080/(617) 626-1590 www.state.ma.us/dfwele/dfw

Michigan Department of Natural Resources, Mason Building, Sixth Floor, PO Box 30028, Lansing, MI 48909 (517) 373-2329 www.michigan.gov/dnr

Minnesota Department of Natural Resources, 500 Lafayette Rd., St. Paul, MN 55155-4040 (888) MINN-DNR/(651) 296-6157 www.dnr.state.mn.us

Mississippi Wildlife, Fisheries and Parks, 1505 Eastover Dr., Jackson, MS 39211-6374 (601) 432-2400 www.mdwfp.com

Missouri Department of Conservation, PO Box 180, (Zip 65102), 2901 W. Truman Blvd., Jefferson City, MO 65109 (573) 751-4115 www.conservation.state.mo.us

Montana Fish, Wildlife and Parks, 1420 E Sixth Ave., PO Box 200701, Helena, MT 59620-0701 (406) 444-2535 www.fwp.state.mt.us

Nevada Department of Wildlife, 1100 Valley Rd., Reno, NV 89512 (775) 688-1500 www.ndow.org

Nebraska Game and Parks Commission, PO Box 30370, 2200 N 33rd St., Lincoln, NE 68503-0370 (402) 471-0641 www.ngps.state.ne.us

New Hampshire Fish and Game Department, 11 Hazen Dr., Concord, NH 03301 (603) 271-3421/2461 www.wildlife.state.nh.us

New Jersey Department of Environmental Protection, Division of Fish and Wildlife, PO Box 400, 501 E State St., 3rd Floor, Trenton, NJ 08625-0400 (609) 292-2965/9192 www.state.nj.us/dep/fgw

New Mexico Department of Game and Fish, PO Box 25112, Santa Fe, NM 87507 (800) 862-9310 www.gmfsh.state.nm.us

New York Department of Environmental Conservation, Division of Fish, Wildlife and Marine Resources, Bureau of Wildlife, 625 Broadway, Albany, NY 12233-4750 (518) 402-8919/8845 www.dec.state.ny.us/website/dfwmr/wildlife

North Carolina Wildlife Resources Commission, 1722 Mail Service Center, Raleigh, NC 27699-1722 (919) 622-4370/(888) 248-6834 www.wildlife.state.nc.us

North Dakota Game and Fish Department, 100 N Bismarck Expy., Bismarck, ND 58501-5095 (701) 328-6300/6335 www.state.nd.us/gnf

Ohio Department of Natural Resources, Division of Wildlife, 1840 Belcher Dr., Columbus, OH 43224-1300 (614) 265-6565 www.dnr.state.oh.us

Oklahoma Department of Wildlife Conservation, PO Box 53465 (Zip Code 73152-3465), 1801 N Lincoln, Oklahoma City, OK 73105 (405) 521-3851/2739 or (800) 223-3333 www.wildlifedepartment.com

Oregon Department of Fish and Wildlife, 3406 Cherry Ave. NE, Salem, OR 97303-4924 (503) 947-6100/6300 www.dfw.state.or.us

Pennsylvania Game Commission, 2001 Elmerton Ave., Harrisburg, PA 17110-9797 (717) 787-2869/2084 www.pgc.state.pa.us

Rhode Island Department of Environmental Management, Division of Fish and Wildlife, 4808 Tower Hill Rd., Wakefield, RI 02879 (401) 789-3094 www.state.ri.us/dem/programs/bnatres/fishwild/index.htm

South Carolina Department of Natural Resources, Wildlife and Freshwater Fisheries, PO Box 167, Columbia, SC 29202 (803) 734-3886 www.dnr.state.sc.us

South Dakota Department of Game, Fish and Parks, Division of Wildlife, 523 E Capitol Ave., Pierre, SD 57501-3182 (605) 773-3485 www.state.sd.us/gfp

Tennessee Wildlife Resources Agency, Wildlife Division, Ellington Agricultural Center, PO Box 40747, Nashville, TN 37204 (615) 781-6610 www.state.tn.us/twra

Texas Parks and Wildlife, 4200 Smith School Rd., Austin, TX 78744 (800) 792-1112/(512) 389 4800 www.tpwd.state.tx.us

Utah Division of Wildlife Resources, PO Box 146301 (Zip Code 84114-6301), 1594 W. North Temple, Salt Lake City, UT 84114 (801) 538-4700 or Recorded Information (877) 592-5169 www.wildlife.utah.gov

Vermont Agency of Natural Resources, Department of Fish and Wildlife, 10 South Building, 103 S Main St., Waterbury, VT 05671-0501 (802) 241-3700 www.anr.state.vt.us

Virginia Department of Game and Inland Fisheries, 4010 W Broad St., Richmond, VA 23230 (804) 367-1000 www.dgif.state.va.us

Washington Department of Fish and Wildlife, Natural Resources Building, 1111 Washington St. SE, Olympia, WA 98501-1091 (360) 902-2200 www.wa.gov/wdfw

West Virginia Division of Natural Resources, 1900 Kanawha Blvd. East, Capitol Complex, Building 3, Room 663, Charleston, WV 25305-0660 (304) 558-3315 www.wvdnr.gov

Wisconsin Department of Natural Resources, PO Box 7921, 101 S Webster St., Madison, WI 53707-7921 (608) 266-2621 www.dnr.state.wi.us

Wyoming Game and Fish, 5400 Bishop Blvd., Cheyenne, WY 82006 (307) 777-4600 www.gf.state.wy.us

US Fish & Wildlife Service

Pacific Region (Region #1), 911 NE 11th Ave., Portland, OR 97232-4181 (503) 231-6128 www.pacific.fws.gov/index.cfm Manages more than 100 wildlife refuges in California, Hawaii, Idaho, Nevada, Oregon, Washington and other Pacific Islands.

Southwest Region (Region #2), PO Box 1306 (Zip Code 87103-1306), 500 Gold Ave. SW, Suite #9019, Albuquerque, NM 87102-3118 (505) 248-7450 www.southwest.fws.gov/ Manages more than 40 wildlife refuges in Arizona, Oklahoma, New Mexico and Texas.

Midwest Region (Region #3), Bishop Henry Whipple Federal Building, 1 Federal Dr., Ft. Snelling, MN 55111 (612) 713-5130 www.midwest.fws.gov Manages 46 wildlife refuges and wetlands areas in Illinois, Indiana, Iowa, Michigan, Minnesota, Missouri, Ohio and Wisconsin.

Southeast Region (Region #4), 1875 Century Blvd., Atlanta, GA 30345 (404) 679-4159 www.southeast.fws.gov Manages 125 wildlife refuges in Alabama, Arkansas, Florida, Georgia, Kentucky, Louisiana, Mississippi, North Carolina, South Carolina, Tennessee, the Commonwealth of Puerto Rico and the US Virgin Islands.

Northeast Region (Region #5), 300 Westgate Center Dr., Hadley, MA 01035-9589 (413) 253-8508/8200 www.northeast.fws.gov Manages 70 wildlife refuges in Connecticut, Delaware, Maine, Maryland, Massachusetts, New Hampshire, New Jersey, New York, Pennsylvania, Rhode Island, Vermont, Virginia and West Virginia.

Mountain-Prairie Region (Region #6), PO Box 25486, 134 Union Blvd., Lakewood, CO 80225 (303) 236-7392/7917 www.mountain-prairie.fws.gov Manages 116 wildlife refuges and 23 wetland districts in Colorado, Kansas, Montana, Nebraska, North Dakota, South Dakota, Utah and Wyoming.

Alaska Region (Region #7), 1011 E Tudor Rd., Anchorage, AK 99503 (907) 786-3545/3354 www.alaska.fws.gov Manages 16 wildlife refuges in Alaska.

Canadian Provinces

Alberta Sustainable Resource Development, Information Centre, Main Floor, 9920 108th St., Edmonton, AB, Canada T5K 2M4 (780) 944-0313 www.gov.ab.ca/srd/fw

British Columbia, Ministry of Water, Land and Air Protection, Fish and Wildlife Recreation and Allocation Branch, PO Box 9374, Stn Prov Govt, Victoria, BC, Canada V8W 9M4 (800) 663-7867/(250) 387-9739 wlapwww.gov.bc.ca/fw/wild/synopsis

Manitoba Conservation, Wildlife and Ecosystem Protection Branch, Box 22-200, Salteaux Crescent, Winnipeg, MB, Canada R3J 3W3 (800) 214-6497/(204) 729-3500 [Map Sales (204) 945-6666] www.gov.mb.ca/conservation/wildlife

New Brunswick Department of Natural Resources, Renewable Resources Division, PO Box 6000 (Zip Code E3B 5H1), Hugh John Flemming Forestry Complex, Room 120, Floor 1, 1350 Regent St., Fredericton, NB, Canada E3C 2G6 (506) 453-2440/3826 www.gnb.ca/0078/index-e.asp

Newfoundland and Labrador Tourism, PO Box 8700, St. John's, NL, Canada A1B 4J6 (800) 563-6353/(709) 729-2830 www.gov.nf.ca/tourism/mainmenu/whattodo/hunting

Northwest Territories Resources, Wildlife and Economic Development, 5th Floor Scotia Bldg., 600, 5102-50th Ave., Yellowknife, NT, Canada (867) 920-8064 www.nwtwildlife.rwed.gov.nt.ca [Licensed Outfitters: NWT Arctic Tourism, PO Box 610, Yellowknife, NT, Canada X1A 2N5 (800) 661-0788]

Nova Scotia Department of Natural Resources, Wildlife Division, PO Box 698, Halifax, NS, Canada B3J 2T9 (902) 434-2351 www.gov.ns.ca/natr/hunt

Ontario Ministry of Natural Resources, Wildlife Section, PO Box 7000, Floor 5, 300 Water St., Peterborough, ON, Canada K9J 8M5 (800) 667-1940/(705) 755-2001 www.mnr.gov.on.ca

Prince Edward Island Department of Environment and Energy, Conservation and Management, Jones Building, 4th Floor, PO Box 2000, 11 Kent St., Charlottetown, PE, Canada C1A 7N8 (866) 368-4683/(902) 368-4683 www.gov.pe/caenveng/cam-info

Quebec Tourism, Societe de la faune et de parc du Quebec, 675 Rene-Levesque Est rez-de-chaussee, Quebec, QC, Canada G1R 5V7 (418) 521-3830 www.fapaq.gouv.qc.ca or www.tourisme.gouv.qc.ca/anglais/activities/chasse

Saskatchewan Environment and Resource Management, Fish and Wildlife Branch, Room 436, 3211 Albert St., Regina, SK, Canada S4S 5W6 (800) 567-4224/(306) 787-2314 [Maps and Aerial Photos (306) 787-2799] www.se.gov.sk.ca/fishwild

Yukon Department of Environment, PO Box 2703, 10 Burns Rd., Whitehorse, YK, Canada Y1A 2C6 (867) 667-5652 www.environmentyukon.gov.yk.ca

Appendix 2 – Deer-R-Edible!

Information from around the world indicates that deer are not only edible, but also exceptionally nutritious. Table A is a comparison between 3-ounce (3 oz) cuts of fallow deer and comparable amounts of beef, chicken and salmon. The information about red deer measures the same. The Irish grocery store chain SuperQuinn (www.superquinn.ie) says, "For weight watchers and anyone wanting to vary a low-cholesterol diet, farmed venison is ideal as a low-fat red meat. Venison, in fact, contains so little fat it is recommended that you cover a joint with streaky bacon and foil to prevent it from drying out before it is fully cooked. Because most of the farmed venison that is sold comes from young animals under the age of 15 months, it is more tender than most meats and needs no special treatment before cooking – unlike more strongly flavored wild venison, which is best marinated."

Based on data from the US Department of Agriculture and published at www.nutritiondata.com, there is good news and bad news about venison. It is rated very high in cholesterol, but the good news is its low sodium content. It is a good source of Thiamin, Vitamin B6, Iron, Phosphorus, Zinc and Copper. It is a very good source of Riboflavin, Niacin and Vitamin B12. (This site's information is rated as Deer USDA below and it is slightly different from other values reported.)

Table A

Meat	Calories	Fat (gm)	Cholesterol (mg)	Protein (gm)
Venison				
USDA	102	3	72	18
leg cut	139	5	62	22
Salmon				
broiled	140	5	60	21
Chicken				
skinless	140	3	72	26
Lamb				
loin	183	8	80	25
Beef				
tenderloin	174	8	72	24
bottom round	189	8	81	27
ground	213	12	84	25
brisket	223	13	77	24
Pork				
shoulder	207	13	82	22
Veal				
cutlet	155	4	112	28

Sources: Fallow deer from a Rancho de la Cuesta, Templeton, CA 11-03, www.farmedvenison.com; red deer from Shaffer Venison Farms, Herndon, PA, www.shafferfarms.com; and the USDA as reported at www.nutritiondata.com.

INDEX